Reiki for Angels

Finally, Reiki explained in clear, indisputable scientific terms that speak to a newer, tech-savvy generation.
– A reader.

C.A. Blaney, Ph.D.

Reiki

For

Angels

Advanced Theory & Practice

C.A. Blaney, Ph.D.

ISBN: 1548119431
ISBN-13: 978-1548119430

DEDICATION

May the message herein help to bring the light of joyful healing to many people.

ACKNOWEDGEMENTS

I acknowledge Albert Einstein for his insightful 'thought experiment' which helps one realize that *accelerating through space in a rocket* feels the same as standing on Earth and *having space (Aether) accelerate through you.*

Much gratitude to John Lyes – artist, musician, co-creatrix and soulmate – who pointed out to me that *the natural flow of fluids was spiral* and thus turned me into a legitimate physicist.

Thanks to all the 'Earth' Angels who chose to come live upon the blue planet to help Mother Earth and her beloved inhabitants regain health and balance.

CONTENTS

Preface   1

1   What is Reiki?   7

2   What is an (Earth) Angel?   17

3   The Beginning of the Universe   25

4   What is Light?   34

5   What is Matter?   51

6   What is Life?   71

7   Resonance, Coherence & Intention   79

8   Reiki Practice For (Earth) Angels   88

About the Author   103

PREFACE

To whom it may concern:

A young teenager named Annie Blane recently submitted a poignant question to the G.O.D. (Galactic Oversight Department). Here is her letter:

"Dear Archangel Meryl, c/o G.O.D.,

I hope all is well. I assume you're off on another urgent pan-galactic mission, given your absence from my 3-D cell phone app for most of senior year.* Hoping to see you at graduation! Now, to the purpose of my letter.

It seems my friends (and actually everyone on this strange Earth planet) all have some sort of ailment – like headaches, depression, anxiety, stomach aches, etc. And the adults are even worse, with more serious diseases. I feel like I want to help – like I'm supposed to help – but I'm not sure how. I'm not a doctor – at least not yet!

I heard Jesus healed the sick by laying on of hands. Is there some trick to that? I mean can I do that? Seems pretty easy, right? I wouldn't need to go to medical school (at least not right away) and no equipment would be needed. Might be fun, too – especially if I helped my friends feel better.

Looking forward to your detailed reply. Missing
you,
Annie Blane, Earth Angel, Level 2

*Refers to a scene in a novel by same author.

Dear Annie Blane,

Thank you for alerting the G.O.D. of your concerns. I
want you to know that Archangel Meryl did read
your letter, and has kindly and promptly forwarded it
to my A.I. (Angelic Inbox), since I, Archangel
Raphaella, am currently overseeing all the healing
activities of the Universe.

My detailed reply to your question is in the form of
this small book, entitled "Reiki for Angels." It will be
delivered to you the next time you enter a bookstore.
It's soothing pink cover shall serve to lure your eyes
towards it. Afterwards, I urge you to go buy a pint of
strawberry ice cream and eat it as you peruse the
pages.

> **NOTE: Feel free to skip straight to the last
> two chapters of this book if you are not in
> the mood to contemplate the creation of the
> universe just yet.**

Alas, the blue planet has spoiled its own nest by
evolving upon it's biosphere a species called Humans.
In your era, the thinking portion of the human brain

is often found to be completely disconnected from the rest of its body (that is, disconnected from the heart and other organs), and disconnected from the Earth, too. So these frontal brain-dominated humans throw their toxic waste onto the Earth and into their own bodies. This is a major cause of the pervasive illnesses and sufferings of which you speak, Annie.

The disconnected human brain, on its own, operates similarly to a soul-less machine. This machine is programmed with outdated evolutionary software, to become the 'tribal leader.' This leads to many additional causes of the pervasive suffering.

The ones who suffer the most are the women, who are pushed into low-hierarchy, slavery roles by the men's forceful aspirations to become the tribal leaders. And the men who don't manage to rise to leadership positions also suffer a lot, with feelings of failure tainted with anger, shame, retribution, inadequacy, and so forth. This stress exacerbates the mind-body separation and leads to bodily disharmony and illness.

The children are sometimes immune to this phenomenon, and therefore we find blessings and inspiration from among them. However, if these children are exposed to this larger 'social' system that has evolved in the last century, they too are misled into brain-body separation, and eventually they also seek to rise to leadership positions. This perpetuates the problem of stress, which takes the ultimate toll on the health of the human (and the health of the planet).

Technologies like radio and television, and more recently the internet, digital entertainment and global marketing, and most poignantly, smart phones – has made this 'worst sort of lie' all-pervasive – that lie of separation and the need to be rich, famous, cool, and powerful. It is the seed of human suffering.

In summary, the frontal cortex portion of the brain is split/separated from the human body and from the planet. This soulless machine (prefrontal cortex) blindly follows instructions from outdated software to 'be the best.' Thus these soulless (split) people hoard possessions and power, at the expense of others, at the expense of their planet, and at the expense of their own bodies which they are 'separated' from.

So you see, Annie, this split-brain situation causes the majority of the human bodily malfunctions that result in suffering and ill-health.

If we use Reiki to help our friends reconnect 'brain-to-body,' as I teach in this book, they might awaken to an improved, healthier lifestyle – first by lessening their stranglehold on the societal lie of having to rise to the top; and second, by eating healthier, thinking healthier, breathing more deeply, and acting in healthier ways. This would remove the toxic load on their bodies, both chemical toxins and mental toxins such as incorrect thought.

And so, it is primarily the mind (split from the body, and partly housed in the 'separated' brain) that must be healed and reunited.

A few preliminary words about the human body:
The human body is the place where the brain, nervous system and mind primarily reside. This body is comprised of these and many other organs which are all in constant, real-time, inter-communication with each other – every organ with every other organ; every cell with every other cell; every mitochondria and every bacterium with every other entity. Much of this intercommunication is transmitted through the piezoelectric and conductive 'connective tissue,' also called the 'fascia.' It is here that the Reiki healing energy will predominantly travel, both through you the healer, and into the healee, in order to transmit the healing information in the form of light and other energetic patterns.

The human body also extends outwardly to one's home, one's neighborhood, city, and ultimately to the entire planet and universe. We are all connected, interconnected, and interdependent. We all co-create one another. This well-understood phenomenon can no longer be overlooked.

And so, Annie Blane (and other seekers and healers), it is the interconnectedness of the mind-body-environment that will be your primary focus as you embark to heal your fellow Earth co-inhabitants. This book attempts to instruct you how to do this properly. It is addressed to you, Annie Blane; however, it also serves as a study guide for all of the Earth Angels and Guardians of the Blue Planet who elected to incarnate upon Planet Earth to help with her survival and longevity.

It is required reading, but you may choose when to read it. There is one exception. If any one of you potential Reiki healers is presented with this book, it is a personal alert from the G.O.D. (most probably from me, Archangel Raphaella, or my dear friend and colleague Archangel Meryl) that you are about to encounter a situation in which your healing hands will be direly needed. We Archangels are, after all, messengers; and we present this book to you when you need to hear our message.

Remember, beloved, that the healer and healee shall both benefit equally. For the compassionate act of healing heals both healer and healee.

Peace and healing light,

Archangel Raphaella
May 30, 2017
Channeled by C.A. Blaney, Texas, USA

1   WHAT IS REIKI?

Reiki is a form of energy healing. Energy healing can be thought of as the application of energy to heal a living organism (as opposed to drugs, herbs, or topicals). Its use dates back thousands of years. Most are aware of the historical figure Jesus, who was reported to heal the sick by a 'laying on of hands.' This is a form of energy healing and is believed by the author to be a form of Reiki healing.

Fast-forward to now.

The term 'Reiki' refers to a specific, modern technique of 'laying on of hands,' and is well known among the many energy healing methods of the 21st century. The term 'Reiki' was first used in Japan in the late 19th century, when a group of Japanese practitioners performed and taught the technique locally. The 'Usui' style of Reiki was brought into the western world in the early 20th century. Now it is taught all over the world. One can learn this technique by taking Reiki classes such as Reiki level I and II, and Master Level classes. More details of the history of Reiki and how it began in Japan and moved to the west may be found at http://www.reiki.org/faq/historyofreiki.html.

Some people discover this healing method without ever taking any classes or hearing about Reiki. It is very natural and intuitive. If you hurt yourself and begin to rub your hands on the hurt area, you are doing self-Reiki. You are taking care of your wound with caring attention and with a sincere, loving desire to help the hurt area feel better. You are also literally applying a form of nourishing, healing energy to your wound – infrared light. So you see, you always knew about Reiki healing ever since you were a child.

Reiki healing energy flows from our hands, and those who practice Reiki healing methods can feel this energy. Most **healees** (clients, friends, etc., whom Reiki is being performed on) also report they can feel the energy flowing into and through them, and often report that it gives them a feeling of bliss. And more recently, this 'energy flow' has been scientifically confirmed.

Dr. James L. Oschman, in his book *Energy Medicine: The Scientific Basis*, teaches the science of 'energy flow' in the human body, and he shows how normalizing and optimizing this energy flow can restore health. In particular, he has measured the **bio**

photons (light emitted by living organisms) emitted from the hands of trained Reiki healers as they perform Reiki healing, and has reported that they emit a high level of coherent infrared light.

Forms of Light Therapy:
Infrared light is the light that is beyond the red light. It is a longer wavelength than red, and it is a gentler ray. Some animals can see it, like bats and snakes. But the human can only see colors: red, orange, yellow, green, turquoise, blue, and violet. You cannot see the infrared; you can only feel it. It feels warm because infrared light rays cause the water molecules in your body to vibrate, and you feel this as thermal heat. But it is not the thermal heat that is responsible for the healing effect. Only some of the infrared is converted to thermal heat. The rest of the infrared light travels deeper into the tissue where it interacts with other body molecules. It interacts with enzymes and other cell components. It helps mitochondria make energy (ATP). It helps your microcapillaries expand (by causing the nitric oxide to increase) and thus helps microcirculation, which itself helps the bloodstream transport nutrients to cells, as well as to remove toxins from cells. And it reduces inflammation. These are just a few examples of the many healing effects of infrared light.

In the 1980's NASA claimed that infrared light was the most important light frequency for human health. Scientists discovered this fact as they researched the effects of light on the human body, because they wanted to make sure that the astronauts got all the healthy light they needed while they were away from the sun, out in the darkness of space. Since then, research has revealed (as stated earlier) that red and infrared light beneficially increases circulation, and reduces pain and inflammation.

In fact, science has confirmed that **we need *all* the colors of light for our health**, not just **red** and **infrared**, and this includes green, blue, and even the 'invisible' infrared and ultraviolet. For example, **ultraviolet** rays can help us produce the nutrient Vitamin D, considered by many modern medical doctors as the most important vitamin. In small doses, **ultraviolet** can boost the immune function. It also kills germs. And **blue** light was shown as early as 1876 to stimulate the glandular system. **Blue** can help babies who are born with jaundice (hyperbilirumenemia) to convert the bilirubin until their liver matures. Placing jaundiced babies under blue lights (or full spectrum sunlight) will visibly change their yellow skin (with too much yellow bilirubin) back to a normal color. **Green** light has also been reported in the literature to catalyze (facilitate) vital enzymatic reactions in the body.

Doctors and sports therapists commonly use pulsed LED devices for their patients to reduce pain, speed healing, treat skin conditions, and more.

These are all forms of 'light therapy,' which is considered a form of energy medicine since 'light' is energy. So we could say that **Reiki is also a form of**

light therapy, since the hands of a Reiki healer emit high levels of coherent infrared light rays.

But **Reiki is much more than just light therapy**. It also has other energetic factors at play. The Reiki healer is sending much more than just infrared photons into the body of the healee. For example: The healer also sends loving intention, and this is more than a wish; it is an electromagnetic pattern emitted by your body and brain, and it can be measured.

Did you know that when you go to the doctor to get an EKG (an electrocardiogram), that *your body's emitted electromagnetic field (EMF)* is being measured? The machine uses this EMF measurement to deduce your heartbeat pattern. Your brain also emits an electromagnetic field that is caused by neurons firing in the different brain regions.

There is a lot of equipment that you can buy that can measure these fields. For example, for a few hundred dollars you can buy a system for measuring the electromagnetic fields that your brain emits, and you can then watch your brain's emitted electromagnetic fields on your smart phone or home computer. You can then try to make the firing patterns more coherent and slower. This process of observing your brainwave firing patterns, and then trying to alter them, is called EEG-biofeedback, and many meditators do this form of biofeedback in order to learn to meditate more quickly and efficiently. Your computer screen shows you how your brain is firing in real time. It shows the amplitude of nerves firing, frequency of nerve firing patterns, location of these patterns, and the coherence of the firing patterns. You can then see that when you become very relaxed and dream-like that your brain's neurons fire much more slowly, in alpha (10-14Hz) or theta (4-9Hz) frequencies. You will see also that the more coherently your brain neurons fire, the happier and more peaceful you feel. 'Coherence' means that the neurons all fire at the same time. They are 'in synch.' That's what a lot of meditators train themselves to do – to have coherent neuronal firing. You don't need fancy equipment to train yourself to have coherent neuronal firing, but some like to buy it, practice EEG-biofeedback, and learn much more quickly.

Coherence is a very healthy state to be in. It is also healthy to slow down the brain firing pattern. It can help the entire body to communicate with itself, which makes all the organs work better. This makes you happier on many levels.

All of these electromagnetic fields that the body emits are related to your mood, your health, your intention, and more. And Reiki healing transmits these energies via your presence, and even more so through your hands, in addition to the infrared photons that were measured by Dr. Oschman.

Imagine you are performing Reiki healing on your client. Your client's body receives your electromagnetic energy patterns from your hands, which are related to your mood, your heartbeat pattern, and your brainwave firing patterns. Your client also receives high levels of infrared photons from your hands. If these infrared photons are coherent, that is a message to your client that you are in a state of calm peace, and that you want to offer support. They can sense whether you care about them or not. It feels very pleasant when we are in the presence of another person who really cares about us. It is called love energy, and it is very, very healing.

But you cannot send healing love energy without proper preparation.

There is a well-known book entitled "The Field" by Lynn McTaggart (2012), which teaches how **we are all connected to each other and the world**. She discusses how modern physics research has concluded we co-create each other, and that no object is a separate thing; no person is separate from other people. We are all connected to, and one with, each other, and the planet as well. If we harm the planet, we harm ourselves. If someone harms another, he harms himself. It is a scientific fact. Modern physics explains this at subatomic levels.

This is explained by considering that every 'thing' is in existence only because of its surroundings. Without the surroundings, that 'thing' would cease to exist. You cannot have black without white. You cannot have love without the concept of its opposite. You cannot have an observed event without the observer, and the observer himself affects the very same universe that contains the observed event. **The very act of observing an event affects what is being observed.** Thus we call it co-creation. The observer affects the observed and vice versa.

The Intention Experiment, also by Lynn McTaggart, goes on to describe how our intention goes a long way in our co-creating the world around us. When we intend something, we generate an electromagnetic field around our bodies that affects the world around us. In later chapters we discuss the various methods McTaggart reports that maximize the power and effectiveness of our intentions – especially with regards to how we might best heal others. For example, it is very important to have a loving intention, and not a negative intention. A negative intention hurts others, hurts the world, and hurts yourself most of all because it is sourced within your own mind/body and thus is a very close-acting force – every cell can feel it strongly.

We will be continuing our discussion of the inter-connectedness of all entities, in the context of Reiki healing, and in the context of the emerging physics of the 21st century. After all, this concept is the source of the information in this book.

On the youtube.com channel *Dr. Blaney Physics*, a new theory is presented (Blaney's Theory of Aetheric Flux) which unifies all the physical forces. That is, all the forces of the universe can be explained using one unified view: That of the fluid nature of the entire universe. The flowing nature of this universal fluid is designated **Aetheric Flux.** Simply put, this universal fluid, Aether, is treated as a fluid (in a Chemical Engineering sense) with a context-dependent 'apparent viscosity' and 'apparent density.' This theory is described in more detail in the next several chapters on Light, Matter, Gravity, and their formation.

Dr. Blaney's Theory of Aetheric Flux, in summary, teaches a useful method to perceive and predict the structure of our Universe. It qualitatively and elegantly explains *every thus-far-measured phenomenon* at all size scales, including all the observable forces: magnetic, electric, strong and weak nuclear forces, and gravity. It also explains the expanding universe and dark matter.

The theory is driven via the consideration of fluid dynamics – that is, how fluids flow on all size scales and at all viscosities, including solids, liquids, gases, plasmas, the zero-point field, and fluids of even lower viscosity down to the zero-viscosity fluid which is the quiescent 'VOID.'

In this book, Blaney presents the theory by beginning with the VOID, and builds a universe from this 'initial' building block. What spontaneously arises from the VOID are two additional building blocks: SPACE and TIME. These three fundamental building blocks form a trilogy: VOID=Father, SPACE=Holy Spirit, and TIME=the Son. This trilogy remains pervasive at all size scales.

Of Note: Blaney presents this theory to physicists as a 'template' of a Unification Theory – showing how the task of *The Unification of the Physical Forces* must be tackled. It has self-consistency and is recursive at all size scales, including those miniscule size scales inaccessible to 'probing and measuring' with our modern scientific instruments.

For the Reiki practitioner, the 'golden nectar' of this theory, e.g. the 'heart of the heart', or crux of this theory, is that when you visualize the Universe in this way, you can more accurately 'see' and 'feel' the Aetheric flux flowing into the top of your head, through your body and into the ground, as well as circulating within you as it flows into every molecule and bio photon within you. Being conscious of the presence of the Aetheric flux flowing into and through you is the first step to understanding Reiki Energy flow. Understanding it on a scientific (physics) level goes a long way in helping the Earth Angel healer to generate optimally-effective healing energy and apply it during Reiki healing.

If you properly create your *intention to heal*, you will then effectively channel 'healing' Aetheric flux into your healee, benefiting them greatly, and insuring no harmful patterns are transmitted. In doing so, you will also greatly benefit yourself with the same 'healing' Aetheric flux as it flows through you, and into the healee.

2 WHAT IS AN EARTH ANGEL?

This book is written for Earth Angels, and you, the reader, are likely one. An Earth Angel is not an Archangel. Let us now discuss each type of 'angel.'

An **Archangel** is made of light (as a first approximation), exists everywhere, and is a messenger of useful information to humans.

An **Earth Angel** is a human being, and is made of both mass and light (although present-day scientists will claim humans are 100 percent mass/matter). The human Earth Angel is a *novice angel-in-training* who incarnated in human form to learn, and to help the human race survive. Earth Angels are sometimes able to receive the messages transmitted by the Archangels.

The scribe of this book, Dr. C.A. Blaney, is an Earth Angel. She has spent 12 years constructing and confirming a Unification Theory which is the heart of this book as it applies to the transmission of Reiki Healing Energy.

However, like all humans, Blaney is burdened with a fearful human ego that has prevented her from sharing this theory for many years – because she has no interest in trying to 'defend' its indisputable truth to the 'conventional'-minded physicists who would love to ridicule any newfangled theory. Rather, Blaney only seeks to use her theory and understanding for the greater good. She isn't really in the mood to enter into a debate with these rigid physicists.

Therefore, seeing this silly ego-based roadblock, I, Archangel Raphaella, female embodiment of the Healing Energy of Light, have stepped in to help Blaney share her useful information to the world, by channeling her own theory through her – but in my own words. I, being an Archangel without the burden of a human ego, personally have no need to justify or prove any aspect of the information discussed here. As Blaney has communicated to me numerous times (and I agreed), the theory is indisputable, and is in fact exactly how Archangels perceive the universe and its forces.

By letting go of fearful judgement and merely being a scribe, Blaney has freed her ego from the transmission of this information, leaving the flow of words to me. She has done the work; all she has to do now is write down what I tell her, as she listens to soothing music.

We Archangels are messengers of information as it evolves and blossoms among all the living entities of the Universe (i.e. humans and other beings). We collect, preserve, and transmit this acquired wisdom and knowledge of the ages using the medium termed the Akashic Field. It is here in the Akashic Field – the complex soup of the seemingly turbulent Aether – that we Archangels reside, in the form of highly ordered and coherent patterns, and with a will and intention of our own. When you, the recipient (in this case our scribe, Blaney) are able to resonate with the informational Aetheric oscillatory patterns we carry, and you can pick up/sense these fields with your empath-sensitive nervous system and fascia, you will benefit from our messages. This is how all information is channeled. Note that the structure of the Akashic Field will be elucidated upon in the chapters that follow.

To complete my description of what an Archangel is, I cannot fail to mention the conventional image of the Archangel as a long-haired and beautiful human-like being wearing a long flowing robe and being lifted up with a mammoth pair of feathered, glistening wings, usually depicted as white (although a famous Archangel in a recent TV series has been depicted with black wings). The wings and even the halo are a very convenient way for a human being to conceive of our presence. After all, the image conveys a larger-than-life being that is comprised of light. This concept, although close, is not precise. In reality, we are highly coherent vibration patterns within the Aetheric field resonances.

Definition:
Akashic Field: the sum total over all of eternity and throughout all of space, of the Aetheric Flux patterns. It is the living, breathing record of our Universe.

We Archangels physically reside in the Akashic Field. We reside 'physically,' not by our mass (we have no mass), but by our light and other coherent Aetheric Flux patterns in the Akashic Field of churning Aether. After all, light is but one form of physical reality in the Aetheric Field. Matter is another physical form, much denser than light (and is in fact 'condensed' light). And our Archangelic Aetheric Flux resonance patterns contain vast volumes of information which we carry in the form of messages to Humans.

We Archangels occupy vast spaces at once. In fact, if you want to get technical and nit-picky about it, even humans occupy vast spaces at once, since both light and mass have waveforms that extend to infinity. But in defense of the 'locality' concept of humans, your human mass waveform packet dies out orders of magnitude closer to your center of gravity than the waveforms of angelic beings. In fact, Archangels are 'smeared' across space, because like light, our Archangelic 'body parts' travel around in the Aether at the 'speed of light' c.

A metaphor of the 'messenger nature' of an Archangel is as follows: Imagine you are standing with your smart phone in the middle of a busy street in New York City. You are expecting a call, so you place yourself in view of a cell phone tower, and then you check the little icon on your phone, confirming that you have a strong signal.

Incidentally, the bee buzzing around the nearby flowers can 'see' all the blinding microwaves being emitted from the myriad of cell phone towers, bouncing around from building to building. To the bee it looks quite chaotic, because the microwave colors shimmer in a confusing pattern of jumbled, wretched chaos. Now, your phone rings. You answer.

"Hello?" you say.
"Darling! I'm just arriving in Tokyo," says your sweetheart, "and it's even more crowded than New York City! Can you believe it?"

Your sweetheart continues telling you all about Tokyo as you reply with many curious questions about the smells, the fashions, the graffiti or lack thereof... you get the picture. Out of all that chaos of microwaves, your smart phone picks up only the transmission of your sweetheart's voice that was meant for you, since she had your code – your cell phone number. In this analogy, the *microwaves* are collectively the Akashic Field, and *the specific set of microwaves transmitting your sweetheart's voice* is the Archangel's voice sending his/her message to you.

An Archangel has the code to your sensory organs. If your 'phone' is on, then you will receive the (cell phone) call from the Archangel. In other words, if your sensory equipment – your nervous system, fascia, and so forth – are primed, aware, receptive, and ready-to-receive, then you will be able to receive, interpret, and transcribe the message sent to and through you by the Archangel. Blaney the scribe of this book is doing just this.

And to wrap up the chapter, we'll say a bit more about Earth Angels.

As discussed earlier, an Earth Angel is a being who incarnates on Earth to help the human race survive. Specifically, an Earth Angel has lived in the 'mass' realm many lifetimes, and has evolved spiritually quite a long way. He/she is well over halfway to 'Bodhisattva'-level – a term for an enlightened being who chooses to return to Earth to help others attain enlightenment – though some Earth Angels are closer to Bodhisattva than others. Scribe Blaney is barely halfway, and is still quite ego-bound as can be seen by her lack of courage and her serious anxiety issues. But it's all as it should be, because the thing about being born an Earth Angel is that you choose to come here to not only help Earth, but you help yourself evolve to Bodhisattva level more quickly, since it is quite a challenging endeavor to live among humans.

Before arriving on Earth, the Earth Angel is specifically trained for living among humans in what are termed 'Purgatory classes.' For example, in *Earth Angel Purgatory Classes*, one learns about humans. In particular, the Earth Angel learns about the human Neurotypical mind, and how it contains outdated, ancient software programs. Thus, sadly, the majority of the human race is still power-hungry with barely a lofty goal, and barely a passion to help the human race. Rather, most humans just want to help themselves and their immediate families. But like all species in their 'teenage' phase of evolution, with a little help in staying alive and avoiding the pitfalls of careless youth, they will survive their 'teen-hood' and evolve into a wiser species, in time.

The Earth Angels are commissioned as volunteers to come and help the 'teenaged' earthlings improve, evolve, and survive. Even more importantly, the Earth Angels are charged with the job of helping preserve Earth. For without a healthy planet, there can be no place for the human race to evolve further. For as vast and abundant as our universe is, there is no possible physical way to get the human race relocated onto another life-supporting planet in it's current 'mass-bound' state of existence. (The nearest life-supporting planet is simply too far away.) The Earth is it. Without that, the Earth vector of life and its corresponding informational evolution and artistic blossoming will vanish.

Summary:
So there you have it. Archangels are messengers of

the accumulated wisdom and knowledge stored in the Akashic Field, are made of Aetheric Oscillatory Patterns that travel through the Aether at the speed of light c, and exist at vast places simultaneously. And Earth Angels are reincarnated [light and mass] human beings, highly localized, highly evolved (but not enlightened yet), who chose to come to Earth to help it survive so that humans might continue to evolve. The Earth Angels are trained beforehand about the peculiarities of the human race they are coming to save.

Note: To learn more about what an Earth Angel is, there is an entire book about the subject entitled *Guardians of the Blue Planet,* also with C.A. Blaney as scribe. It is the story of four young Earth Angels, and how an Archangel named Meryl came to inform them of their status and duties. It is also a love story.

3 THE BEGINNING OF THE UNIVERSE

In Chapter 1 it was revealed that Reiki healers emitted light from their hands when performing Reiki healing – infrared light to be exact. Logically, to fully understand Reiki, one needs to know what light is.

What is light?

To answer that question, we first must understand what light is made of. Light is made of Aetheric flux in a particular pattern of flow. And to understand what Aetheric flux is, we must go even deeper – to the very beginning of the universe.

According to the Blaney Theory of Aetheric Flux (and perhaps according to many others as well), before anything existed, there was only the VOID. This is the undefinable nothingness that preceded any consciousness or words, thus the only word that is fitting for it is the VOID. (Nothingness.) Blaney, trained extensively in chemical engineering fluid dynamics and physics, explains in her own view that the VOID was actually a fluid of zero viscosity, zero density and zero inertia, and thus it would take 'zero' force to move it. So this zero density fluid inevitably began to move. And it moved with infinite velocity, in all directions, at all size scales. Since this infinite velocity existed everywhere in every direction, we thus define an unusual and temporary 'initial' multidimensional vector field with the following properties: infinite velocity, infinite curl, infinite disorder (infinite entropy), and infinite extension (exists over all 3-D space), at time equals zero. This is our starting point, called the 'initial condition.' It corresponds with what physicists have historically called the 'big bang.'

To characterize our 'big bang' state, we say it began with only one building block (the quiescent VOID) which was infinitely unstable. Thus, this VOID 'quickly' and instantaneously formed into a 'something' that was *more* stable – something moving. And thus, it changed itself into *something else*. It *changed* (since that is what unstable things do – they change). At the instant of this initial change, two more building blocks were formed out of this change. They were SPACE and TIME.

Why SPACE and TIME?

Well, for **movement** to occur, there must also exist a **place** in which to move around in, thus, SPACE has sprung into existence. And for **change** to occur, there must also occur a **timeframe** in which that change exists. That timeframe is a sequence of *'states of things' with 'identities'* that differ from one another in some way. And so TIME has sprung into existence.

Since the VOID is no longer 'nothingness' we must now rename it. Why is it no longer 'nothingness?" It is because now there exist both SPACE and TIME, in which this 'nothingness' flows, therefore it is no longer nothingness, but a 'something-ness' that flows, and this 'flowing' something-ness is given a specific and useful name by Dr. Blaney that dignifies its worthy existence: AETHER.

The reason Blaney has spelled it with the 'A' is to clarify that it is not the archaic 20th century 'ether' that was regularly poo-poo'ed by the ruling physicists who were loath to admit it's existence all. It is of note that Albert Einstein himself, in his book *Relativity: a simple explanation that anyone can understand*, declared that 'ether must exist as a medium in which to carry the forces of gravity,' which is precisely true. Thus, the Blaney Theory of Aetheric Flux can be considered a direct extension of Einstein's great work, the General Theory of Relativity, applied to very small and very large distances and time scales. The first two letters of AETHER bring this beloved teacher to mind by beginning with his initials, A.E.

Blaney claims that the 'proof' as to the non-existence of an 'ether,' offered by the famous Michelson-Morley experiment, is just plain wrong, due to the archaic tools they had in their laboratories, unable to pick up the subtle wind of this real and turbulent Aether. These hob-knobbing physicists can laugh all they want at Blaney for her bold claim that 'Aether is real stuff, and if measured properly would show a resistance to flow, an inertia, and a gravitational field, due to its infinitely nested twisting and turning turbulent movements' – for if those hob-knobbers read the latest literature in Physics, they would realize it has long been proven that the zero-point field of the vacuum of free space is filled with movement, information, and energy, which is the Aether's infinitely turbulent primordial substance churning uncontrollably at all size scales.

But none of those hob-knobbers have the inclination to read about Reiki anyway, and so we are a close knit bunch of 'in the know' readers whose secret lies safe within these pages.

Herein are the trinity of building blocks of our Universe: The AETHER, and the SPACE and TIME in which it flows.

How can we build a full universe with these three most basic primal building blocks?

First, we must contemplate how this Aether will flow in Space and Time. It is a fluid. We already know all about fluids, because we live among many fluids. Honey is a very viscous and dense fluid and we know how it flows. Water flows even faster, and air faster, still. But these fluids don't flow all that differently.

As we look at all the various fluids around us, and we continue to look at fluids with less and less density, and less and less viscosity, we see there are many similarities. They always seem to flow in curved paths – i.e. consider the curved flow patterns of tornadoes, hurricanes, whirlpools, spirals, and so forth. It is because no fluid particle is alone, but it is among sister and brother fluid particles. It has to flow around its sisters and brothers. And it interacts with each one as it passes, exchanging information and competing for the local resources. Observing carefully, we see that the natural way to flow is into a spiral.

Even the least viscous fluid known, the super cooled Bose-Einstein Condensate fluid (BEC), flows in spiral form – specifically, tiny vortices have been observed right before our very eyes, despite our crude equipment.

And you don't have to be infinitely small to know how Aether will flow at even smaller and smaller size scales. It will flow just like all fluids flow: in spirals.

We, the theoretical physicists of the 21st century, have the information and tools we need to predict the 'apparent' viscosity, density/gravitational properties/dark energy, and inertia, of this turbulent Aether (also termed the zero-point field). We have mathematics (The Navier-Stokes equations, Maxwell's Equations, and Fractal Mathematics) and huge computers that can calculate down to any size-scale we desire. Even better, we can use calculus to exactly predict the apparent viscosity and energy density of the zero-point field, by calculating the limit of 'bulk' viscosity of the local Aether as the [viscosity and density of the quiescent Aether] both approach zero.

Everything can be deduced from the flow of this primordial Aether in Space and Time. And not only does the Aether flow in a curved path, a spiral path, at smaller and smaller levels – even at levels infinitely smaller than Plank's length – but it flows in this way at large scales too. As above, so below. We can see it with our own eyes.

Looking around us we see that the electron in the atom has a spin. And the Bose-Einstein condensate spins in a vortex. And then there is the spinning, spiral flow of blood in the veins and arteries. Water flows down the drain in a spiral pattern. And larger fluids like the atmosphere also flow in a spiral pattern, like the vortex of the tornado and the water spout. And even the vast galaxy is slowly flowing in a spiral pattern. So we know that all fluids, large and small, flow in a spiral pattern.

Every size scale has [a stable vortex that lasts a long time]. The tornado lasts sometimes for a few minutes. It concentrates its energy at its tip. Its tip travels down from the sky. It is filled with debris (i.e. cows, bicycles, and other debris).

As above, so below. Similarly, at a very tiny size scale on the order of Plank's length, there is a very tiny vortex that forms as well, out of the ubiquitous turbulent Aether (out of the zero-point field). It is a photon of light. It has its energy also concentrated in *its* tip, and it travels towards its tip like the tornado. It is not exactly the same as the tornado, but it has debris in it like the tornado, and this debris comprises yet ever-smaller tornadoes – at even smaller size scales. These little tornadoes, these vortex patterns, exist at all size scales. These nested vortices are everywhere, large and small, and they are there no matter how small you go.

There is no 'smallness' you can shrink to, to find nothingness. There will always be the smaller vortices flowing to and fro, comprising the Aetheric flow patterns. And likewise, no matter how big you go, the vortices will be there.

As below, so above. The Milky Way Galaxy is a big spiral caused by inwardly spiraling Aetheric flow, and it has debris in it too, and we are part of that debris. The Aether flows *spirally inwardly* into the center of the galaxy. Since it carries with it any debris in its path, it gives rise to the spiral placement of the stars.

Aether flows spirally inwardly into all matter and light, and in fact into all the vortices at all size scales. This inward spiraling flow of the Aether is balanced by an equal and opposite outward flow, which explains why we observe the universe to be expanding 'out there.' And the inward flow of the Aether continues at the very smallest size scales, all the way down to infinitely small dimensions (much less than Plank's length, and *so very* tiny that we could never hope to measure it at those small sizes). All those vortices are pulling the Aether inwardly, and this ubiquitous inwardly-flowing Aether is actually an *accelerating* Aether (which is just gravity, as will be explained soon). It is what gives rise to the observed 'dark energy' that appears to be everywhere. This inwardly flowing Aether, this dark energy, this gravitational pull, would be expected to exist in higher quantity in the regions of space that were more turbulent, such as in the regions of space in the interstices of the galaxies' planets and stars. This agrees with experimental data, where it is indeed observed that 'dark energy levels' are much more concentrated in the galaxy's interstices (as compared to the vast quiescent space between galaxies).

Inward Flow: Why does the Aether that flows in a spiral pattern flow 'inwardly.' What does that mean, exactly? We are used to dimensions such as up, down, left, right, forward, and backwards, and this defines three dimensional space. But within this 3D space one can also have inward and outward flow – that is, radially inward and radially outward flow. The most simplified way to envision inward flow is to consider the following analogy: Imagine the water flowing down the sink's drain. The water on the outside flows into a smaller and smaller circular path as it exits the sink and enters the pipe. It is flowing inwardly.

A more complex but more accurate view of inwardly-flowing fluid is to imagine the same vortex, but this time it is flowing into a circle, its tip overlapping its tail. The surrounding fluid continues to flow inwardly into such a vortex flow pattern. But since the vortex is now constrained to a circle, then from the outside one sees an overall inwardly flowing fluid.

To explain further: The circular vortex can be envisioned as a donut-shaped sinkhole, forever sucking in the outer fluid. From a distance it looks like a black hole. It is. And **inside the black hole is a toroidal-shaped spiral flow pattern that goes around and around. There is no singularity.** This is how gravity works.

For example, the earth, comprised of myriad of these toroidal-shaped donuts, forever pulls in the outer Aether. This inwardly accelerating Aether, which accelerates from 'out there' into the Earth's core, pulls things along with it, including you, as it holds you onto Earth's surface.

Next you may ask, What makes light? What makes mass? What is the nature of Gravity and other forces? I will now answer these questions in detail in the next few chapters.

4 WHAT IS LIGHT?

As the ubiquitous turbulent Aether flows, there emerge many random flow patterns, some of which are stable. To better understand it's flow patterns, just look at the base of a turbulent waterfall. As the strong torrent of water lands into the receiving pool, it disturbs the receiving pool such that the surface of the pool will move a lot. You will see many random flow patterns come and go as the surface waves react to the waterfall. There will be a lot of spiraling movements of the water that each last a fraction of a second. But the flow is not stable and so these little whirlpools quickly dissipate their momentum onto the surrounding water. But on a rare occasion, you may see a stable whirlpool form that lasts and lasts, as the water flows into it, and through it, and then flows deeper into the pool. It's a vortex.

In a stream of water flowing over the rocks, there are

a lot of stable vortices, because the water that flows in to the vortex has a definite place to go, and a place to leave, and there is always new water coming in, which flows in the same pattern as the water before it.

A stable vortex can also form in the middle of the ocean. If there is enough movement of the seawater, sooner or later this simple form of life will be born – this semi-stable vortex or whirlpool – and it will live a while, taking in the water from its surroundings, like food, and then letting it go as it takes in more water.

Looking up at a stormy sky, you might occasionally see a tornado touch down, another semi-stable vortex, this one made up of air. Like the water whirlpool, the air tornado is also filled with the particles that are carried in the fluid that flows into it. The particles are part of the fluid, and give the fluid its properties. A tornado with very pure air will have different properties than a tornado filled with tree branches and rocks. The one with the rocks will have more damaging (energetic) effects on you if you interact with it.

If you burn incense and carefully study the smoke as it rises up, you see many complex flow patterns, but they are all spiral. The flow is never in a straight line, because the smoke is not rising up alone. It is always surrounded by moving air molecules that force the smoke to curve around. (Exception: if the air is perfectly still, the hot smoke will appear to rise straight up for a bit; however, on a microscopic level there is some interaction with the room air, and some flow curvature, albeit not visibly observable.)

If you are in a crowd of people, that is a sort of fluid medium, and each person is like a molecule of that fluid. If you want to run to the other side of the crowd you can never go in a straight line. You must go around your brothers and sisters. You are not alone, so your path will be very curved. There is no being or thing that is alone. We are all around each other, and so we all interact with and thus co-create one another.

There is not any fluid in the universe that is completely empty. Nothing is ever alone or in isolation. Even the vacuum of space is filled with unimaginably tiny vortices that live only for a tiny fraction of a second in our timeframe, but there are very, very many of these, so at any one instant there are an uncountable collection of little curling flows inside the Aether.

For any single Aetheric spiral flow pattern, there are many smaller flow patterns inside it. Physicists call this soup (of infinitely nested spiral flow patterns) the 'zero-point energy field,' abbreviated as ZPE or ZPF. It is called this because no matter how much you cool a vacuum – even to the lowest possible temperature of zero degrees Kelvin, where no more 'measurable' black body radiation is emitted – there is still this small scale Aetheric movement. 'Zero point' means the point where temperature is exactly measured to be zero degrees Kelvin. The spiral flows that make up the super-low viscosity fluid called the .Aether (ZPF, ZPE) is what we are made of. This Aether writhes with movement and life, just like at the base of the waterfall or on the surface of the ocean.

Since the spiral flows of this Aetheric fluid are infinitely nested at all size scales, the 'bulk' viscosity is not zero anymore. Mathematically, if you calculate the viscosity, it looks like you are *multiplying zero by infinity* to get a non-zero, finite number. This happens all the time in mathematics, and we use this math to imagine, understand, and predict our universe. It appears to work just fine in predicting how things work.

Note that you can never prove the absolute existence of the building blocks of the universe, because you, the person trying to do the proving, are made up of these building blocks. Gödel's famous theorem talks about this – how you can never mathematically prove anything fully. All math students understand this fact. That is why we talk about theories, not as facts, but as useful ways to understand the universe in ways that allow useful predictions that allow you to invent, build, and improve life.

So, imagine you are the size of a sub-atomic particle, looking at the turbulent Aether (the zero-point field) flowing all around you. You will see vortices popping into existence all around, most of them vanishing and dissolving back into the soup, but some remaining.

Of the vortices that remain, these are called 'stable vortices' since they are of such a form as to last a long time. The ones that are the size scale of Plank's length (Blaney's conjecture) are what we scientists observe to be 'photons' of light. For any one of these vortices that form, if you rewind time a bit, you'll notice that, out of the turbulent chaos, whenever a stable vortex arises in the Aether, there will arise a complete set of equal and opposite vortices, each with opposite rotational inertias and opposite linear inertias. Summed together, the energetic components of these two 'twin' vector fields would exactly cancel. This symmetrical set of vortices, which can be expressed mathematically as a single time-variant vector field (called the *twin photons' Aetheric Acceleration Vector Field pattern*) may be expressed as follows:

$$\mathbf{y_{twins}} = f_2(x, y, z, t)$$

These twin photons will fly away from one another in opposite directions, and Blaney calls these vortices 'twin photons' since they were birthed at the same instant, location, and from the same information. Again, these vortices are photons of light. Blaney postulates they will be entangled, forever in communication with one another until the Aetheric connection is disturbed (i.e. if one is sucked into a black hole, or converted into matter, or some other disconnecting phenomenon) – and future research will confirm this (or not). This postulation arises from the famous Bell's Theorem, and 'entangled' particles.

Until the connection of these 'entangled' photons is broken, the equation for the *twin photons' Aetheric Acceleration Vector Field* pattern presented above will constrain them in the entangled state.

This Aetheric flux vector field pattern, y_{twins}, that co-creates this set of twin vortices (or quadruplet or sextuplet vortices) will exist as a vector field that extends out into the universe forever and in all directions. The vector field arrows at each point, x, y, and z, at each instant of time, t, represent the direction and magnitude of the Aetheric acceleration contribution of that photon, at that point in time.

We just discussed the vector field pattern for a set of twin vortex/photons, but you can also express the vector field pattern for a single photon, without including its twin, and this is called the *single photon Aetheric Acceleration Vector Field pattern*. It is expressed as follows:

$$y_{single} = f_1(x,y,z,t)$$

where the mathematical 'origin' of the vector field y_{single} travels (in general) with the observer of the photon.

However, if the mathematical 'origin' of the vector field y_{single} is allowed to travel with the photon at the speed of light, it will no longer be time-variant. This simplifies the mathematics.

$$y_{single} = f_1(x,y,z)$$

For example, as a photon flies past an observing person who is stationary, its 'constant' *Aetheric Acceleration Vector Field pattern* follows this photon at the speed of light, from the point of view of the stationary observer. More information on the photon's 'constant' *Aetheric Acceleration Vector Field pattern* (which travels with the photon) will follow.

These vortices are self-propelled soliton-type waves that just keep moving, the pressurized tip being propelled by the 'uber-high-vacuum' tail, and they will just keep moving along the turbulent Aether forever and ever until one or both are stopped, destroyed, annihilated, transformed, joined, conjoined, or otherwise interacted with.

In summary, the vortex described above (one of the set of photon twins) that emerges out of the Aether, is what a single photon of light is. This light would form in abundance when the Aether was in a turbulent, highly energetic state, such as during the conditions of the Big Bang. This is what is meant when humans write the following: God said 'let there be light.' At the moment the VOID became turbulent AETHER, a lot of light was formed, and this is the same light we see today, all around us. It was created at the instant of the Big Bang, and shortly thereafter.

How does the photon's *vortex flow pattern* actually form, from a fluid-flow perspective?

Creation of Light: In the naturally twisting flow of the Aether, a vortex naturally begins to be formed as the Aether flows in a curved path. The flow is 'inward.' *Why does it flow in an inwardly curling spiral?* It flows inwardly because after a region of Aether goes around in a full circle, it must avoid the trail of Aether it is dragging behind it. If it does not alter its course, it will flow right into its own tail and annihilate itself. However, if it avoids the fluid being dragged along its circular path, its flow can continue. If the moving Aether manages to avoid its own tail, by flowing into a smaller diameter circle, it can still continue to flow.

As the region of Aether flows around its circular path yet another time, the same thing happens, and it's radius of curvature decreases again. And so it keeps flowing in an inward spiral superimposed upon a two-dimensional plane.

Soon, however, as the flowing Aether's radius of curvature becomes ever-smaller, there is too much energy and inertia to continue going *spirally inwardly upon a 2-dimensional plane –* since *the circular area available to collect the inwardly flowing Aether* is limited. When this happens, the flowing Aether is forced to flow in a direction perpendicular to the 2-D plane. So in addition to flowing spirally inwardly, it now flows (to use simplified terms) sideways to the left and sideways to the right. Otherwise it would have nowhere to go. It is the only way it can go. This is how the turbulent Aether makes a pair of vortices that shoot out in opposite directions.

This is a simplified way to visualize the formation of accelerating Aetheric flow that produces a pair of stable vortices. As stated earlier, these paired vortices are 'entangled' with one another.

Viscosity: The above discourse addresses the formation of a photon. It assumes the *flowing Aetheric fluid* has a non-zero (albeit very miniscule) viscosity. This viscosity is caused by the nature of 'the vacuum of space', i.e. zero point field (ZPF). That is, the ZPF is comprised of myriad of smaller, nested whorls and vortices, and other *'inwardly spiraling' flow patterns* of the Aether, causing a summation of gyroscopic forces (due to nested levels of fluid rotation) and, thus, inertia.

"Faerie Dust": This is a technical term for all the 'infinitely nested flow entities' within the ZPF, which give the ZPF it's inertial and viscous flow properties. These Faerie Dust entities, all of which are inwardly spiraling accelerating Aetheric flow patterns, are collectively termed 'Faerie Dust particles' by the author, since they often pop into and out of existence – much like glitter flickering in the light. These 'Faerie Dust' particles, some extremely short lived, are 'dragged along' by the local accelerating Aether, each particle forming an imaginary 'streamline' that traces its path of travel in space and time.

Note: Blaney uses the term 'Faerie Dust' to not only depict its glittering nature, but also to include the consecutive letters 'ae' in acknowledgement of Albert Einstein. This present thesis is a continuation of Einstein's 20th century General Theory of Relativity, but at sub-atomic scales. (Einstein's concept of the 'accelerating ether,' as he called it, was his penultimate inspiration that lead to his famous thought experiments, that in turn gave birth to the GTOR. From there Blaney asks what happens at tiny size scales, gets rid of the singularities in the chapter on Mass, and explains the physical forces with the acceleration of the Aether as well as it's curl.)

Blaney postulates that Faerie Dust gives rise to what physicists call 'dark matter' because the net observable result of Faerie Dust is a bulk inwardly-accelerating flow of the local Aether *into* the ubiquitous Faerie Dust. This *Faerie Dust-induced* inwardly-accelerating Aether is just gravity.

More specifically, Faerie Dust causes the *effect* of gravity by dragging along with it any inertial object in its path. It is termed 'dark matter' by physicists, due to its nature of being short lived, tiny, and thus not observable by any of the current high-tech equipment available in the early part of the 21st century. However it's net effect *is* observable, in that the overall presence of *bulk inward acceleration of Aether* is seen in the trajectories of large astronomical objects which appear effected by *more of a gravitational effect than can be explained* by observable planets, moons, asteroid belts, stars, and so forth.

In support of Faerie Dust, there is an abundance of concrete evidence of the turbulent Zero Point Field's high energy content as reported in myriad peer reviewed physics publications, and is considered well-accepted and deemed a reality by current schools of thought. 'Empty space' is not really empty at all.

The Faerie Dust itself, with its nested levels of curved Aetheric flow and likewise its nested levels of gyroscopic inertia, gives all bulk fluids (the ZPF included) and objects their observed inertia, mass, and gravitational properties.

"Angel View" of photon. Imagine you are an Archangel made of light, and you are traveling alongside the photon at the speed of light, c. What do you see? You see that the photon's tip contains inwardly-twisting, accelerating Aether of a very high magnitude, both in the inwardly rotating velocity (the angular velocity) as well as in the linear velocity (causing the photon to reach terminal velocity c, the speed of light). The surrounding local Aether continues to flow into the photon's vortex. And just like the tornado which sucks up anything in its path, the photon does too, sucking in Faerie Dust from every direction.

Similarly to the tornado, the highest acceleration in the photon is at its tip. Specifically, the photon's Aetheric Flow Vector Field possesses very high first and second derivatives (of the hypothetical Aetheric velocity), at its tip.

A note on the derivatives: The Aetheric acceleration is the first derivative of the Aetheric Velocity. The Aetheric Curl is the second derivative. Again, both are very high at the tip of the photon. This is part of the mathematics of the *Aetheric Acceleration Vector Field* that describes the Aetheric Flux Pattern of the photon.

Note: The Aetheric 'Velocity' is, for our purposes, not a measurable value, but a hypothetical one. This is because it represents the velocity of the zero-viscosity, zero density fluid of the VOID. However, when this VOID 'fluid' flows in its madly chaotic way, even though its velocity approaches infinity, it's acceleration is tamer, and can be expressed mathematically as a finite value; therefore it is the acceleration vector field that is the useful tool to describe the properties of the photon.

All in all, the turbulent VOID forms a *non-zero, non-infinitely-accelerating Aether* (ZPF) that makes up light and matter. (We discuss matter in the next chapter.)

Tip of Photon: Since so much Aether accelerates into the tip of the photon, the tip is very turbulent and thus very full of smaller nested vortices, and so there is more inertia, more density, and more energy in the tip. As the tip moves at the speed of light across space, it pulls the Aether into it. In other words, the surrounding Aether accelerates into the photon's tip.

Tail of Photon: The tail of the photon has a lot of its Aether sucked out of itself into the tip, and this forms a region of low inertia, low density, and low energy at the tail of the photon. You can think of the photon as a twisted bundle of dense Aether at the tip, and a tail of very low density, lacking in turbulent Aether. In fact, the tail of the photon is so empty, so low in Aetheric density that it begins to approach the quietude of the quiescent VOID that only existed before the Big Bang began.

Advanced Comment: A Photon can be thought of as a vortex of the quiescent void (as expressed by the photon's *Aetheric Acceleration Vector Field*) superimposed upon the *ZPF which is filled with Faerie Dust, in which* each particle of Faerie Dust has its own *Aetheric Acceleration Vector Field*. The resulting meta-structure is very complex, but in its simplified form, each particle of Faerie Dust is approximated by a mass particle with a finite lifetime. This simplified view was described in the above paragraphs, as a *vortex filled with debris*, altogether travelling at a terminal velocity c. For those physicists and metaphysicists with enough time and diligence to think it through, this is the only way the human brain can construct a model for how 'objects' can arise out of the void – especially due to the fact that the human brain stacks information in three dimensions. with a memory to allow for storage of sequential events giving rise to the flow of time.

Faeries: Let us imagine for now that we are Faeries

(a technical term) made of mass and mass-like entities, hanging out in outer space – sort of hovering, but never flying very fast – observing the properties of photons as they fly past us at the speed of light c. The energy density of the Aetheric Field all around us (the zero-point field) is some average nonzero value, which we will call A, in units of energy per volume.

A = energy density of the ZPF free vacuum of space

As a photon flies by, we will see that it's tip region has an Aetheric Field density higher than A, and its tail region has an Aetheric Field density lower than A. If you plot the (average, local) Aetheric Field density from the tip of the photon to the tail of the photon, you will get a fast rise in density at the tip, then a gradual decline to A (average density of the regional ZPF) in the middle of the photon, and then a dip in density at the tail of the photon (to near zero), and then in the region called the 'wake' of the photon, it slowly and eventually approaches A once again. There will be a ripple effect at the tail of the photon as the Aether rushes in, overfills it, and becomes a slight vacuum once again, eventually (but quickly) returning to average density A. Think of an echo that quickly dies out.

This 'waveform' is a type of soliton wave. It has a sine wave shape, with one high density region followed by one low density region, then (as a first approximation) back to average density. The tip of the photon is very, very dense in Aetheric energy density and in corresponding energetic Aetheric turbulence, and the tail is very, very non-dense. It is this energy-pressure gradient that propels the soliton wave (in this case a photon) indefinitely along free space. The vacuum of the tail is pushed along – actually, it is quickly 'filled in' by – the surrounding ZPF pressure.

You may not think the surrounding ZPF pressure is high, since it is the same pressure (and same energy density) throughout the local average Aetheric soup of the 'ZPF vacuum of free space'. But it is a lot higher pressure than **the super-duper vacuum of the photon's tail.** So, that *higher-pressure Aether* flows quickly into the vacuum of the photon's tail. It is the same way all pressure waves propagate. In this case, it is mostly explained by **Fickian type** diffusion, which is based on statistical probabilities of where the Faerie Dust particles/entities will flow (from regions of high concentration to regions of low concentration).

The photon's Aetheric Field Energy Density 'plot' or 'graph' just discussed, which forms the soliton-type wave, is really a crude simplification. In reality, the photon's *Aetheric Acceleration Vector Field pattern* is rotating either clockwise or counterclockwise around the axis of the photon's trajectory. The Faerie Dust particles of the ZPF will be sucked into the passing photon and then travel along *with* that photon. It turns out its streamline is defined by the Aetheric Acceleration Vector Field of the photon, which follows the shape of a 2-D golden spiral (mathematical term), superimposed upon a perpendicular accelerating linear component that points in the direction of the photon's travel.

Youtube.com channel *'Dr. Blaney Physics'* shows streamlines of Faerie Dust particles 'caught' by a local, passing photon. The Faerie Dust's path begins slowly at large distances, spirals slowly inward (towards the photon), then faster as it approaches the photon's backbone, around and around it goes, faster, faster, following a golden spiral path. Superimposed upon this inwardly spiraling motion is a flow path that is in the linear direction of the photon's tip. The Faerie Dust particle's path thus curves into a tighter and tighter path, going faster and faster, both in angular velocity (around the axis of photon travel) and in linear velocity (towards the photon's tip).

The Faerie Dust particle's path reveals the streamlines within the photon's Aetheric acceleration Vector Field. When the Faerie Dust particle becomes trapped in the photon's *Aetheric Acceleration Vector Field*, it follows a streamline/path as described earlier, inwardly spiraling into a 2-D golden spiral. While maintaining the spiral movement, it also gradually accelerates in a direction perpendicular to the plane of the golden spiral. The result is a beautiful curved cone shape.

Speed of Light: The tip of the photon (and all the trapped Faerie Dust inside it) cannot travel faster than a particular limiting velocity – the speed of light,

c. This limiting velocity is caused by all the competing flow of the local turbulent Aether – which is also flowing into surrounding zero point field entities (that is, into the ZPF's myriad whorls, swirls, and smaller-scale vortices, e.g. into the Faerie Dust). From the photon's point of view, these *competing ZPF Aether-sucking entities* (the Faerie Dust particles) are flowing *against* the photon at *minus the speed of light c*, thus pulling the photon seemingly backwards with their gravitational effect (backwards accelerating Aether). Thus, the photon can never fully accelerate beyond its terminal velocity c.

Recall again that our teacher, Albert Einstein, first taught the concept of an accelerating 'ether' being equivalent to gravity. In his famous thought experiment he postulated, correctly, that **accelerating through space (Aether) was equivalent to having space (Aether) accelerate through you.** Since photons have Aether accelerating into them, they have gravity. The only reason it's difficult to measure the gravity of the photon is that it's so spread out. We simply can't 'hold a photon still' for a long enough time to make the measurement.

In the next chapter we discuss how light, when condensed, forms a more localized entity called mass, and whose 'inwardly accelerating' is localized, and thus measurable as gravity.

5 WHAT IS MATTER?

Particle or fluid?

We humans on Earth have historically viewed the universe as one giant empty space filled with particles (atoms), as well as these mysterious things called light waves, also often thought of as particles. Historically, every time we split the 'atom' we seemed to get ever-smaller entities, which we called (and still call) sub-atomic 'particles.' Split those, and we get yet smaller entities. When will it end?

However, if you become very tiny and look deeply into those above-mentioned sub-atomic particles, the author asserts that you will discover that they are all actually comprised of flowing (accelerating) Aetheric fluid. It is the flow pattern of that Aether that defines the properties of that sub atomic particle. All *Aetheric acceleration flow patterns* can be described by an *Aetheric Acceleration Vector Field*. We have discussed the *Aetheric acceleration Vector Field* of the photon in the previous chapter.

A *mass* entity has a different, more compact *Aetheric acceleration flow pattern* than a *light* entity. For example, a sub atomic particle called an **electron** appears to be a compact 'particle of mass' that possesses a measurable amount of gravity, as well as a negative electric charge. Yet if you look closely, the author asserts that you will discover it, too, has a specific *Aetheric acceleration Vector Field* unique to all electrons. This vector field will be discussed here.

In fact, every stable entity thought to be a 'particle' is actually an *Aetheric flow pattern* with a corresponding *Aetheric acceleration Vector Field* that defines and expresses that flow pattern.

Even unstable 'entities' that pop into and out of existence in fractions of a picosecond have a flow pattern, but the pattern is extremely transient, and dies out. On the other hand, a photon, and a mass entity like an electron, each have their own unique Vector Field which remains constant over time and follows the photon or electron wherever it goes. If the entity (photon or electron) is absorbed into another larger entity, the individual pattern remains but it also combines with the greater pattern forming a new meta-pattern that defines the larger entity (i.e. an electron-proton pair that makes up an atom of hydrogen.)

The electron particle turns out to be no more of a

particle than a photon is a particle, or than a tornado is a particle. One could *call* a tornado a particle, but if you could safely enter the tornado, you would see it's mostly fluid with smaller debris inside it, and that debris looks like smaller particles. But the debris is also just as fluid-like as the tornado that contains it. If you shrunk yourself further and entered a particle among the tornadic debris, you'd find it too comprised a flow pattern of Aetheric acceleration, and would also be filled with even smaller debris – ad infinitum. Alternatively, if you slice up the tornado, it will dissipate into random turbulence. Similarly, if you could slice a photon, it too would dissipate into smaller (fluid-based) entities. If you slice an electron or other forms or groupings of 'matter,' those too will split into smaller fluid-based Aetheric flow entities, some condensed and localized into a small volume (and appearing very much like solid matter), and others being vortices (and appearing very wave-like), and still others which dissipate into still smaller 'debris' which are fluid-based as well.

The entire universe from big to small is ultimately 'fluid' and made of the primal building blocks of moving AETHER in SPACE and TIME. No matter how small you can shrink yourself, you will see anything you 'thought' was a particle is actually a flow pattern of the Accelerating Aether filled with yet smaller patterns of Accelerating Aether, each of which contain nested flow patterns within, ad infinitum.

What type of Aetheric Flow pattern makes up an

electron?

The following is a thought experiment which describes what an electron is. Imagine you are no longer a human made of mass, but instead *imagine you're an Archangel made of light and traveling alongside a photon.* You reach out to grab the photon, holding its head (the tip) with your right hand and its tail with your left hand, and then you bend it into a circle so that it's tip touches its own tail. What would happen?

Recall from the previous chapter on light that its head is vigorously causing the Aether to accelerate into it, and when this 'Aether-sucking tip' sees its own tail, it sucks that in too. The tail is thus sucked into the head. The *Aetheric acceleration Vector Field* of the photon's tip is superimposed upon the *Aetheric acceleration Vector Field* of the photon's tail. In fact, the photon's entire, infinitely-extended Vector Field, normally existing as a cone-shaped entity in a 3-D Euclidian Grid, is now bent in a circle and superimposed upon itself. The tip continues traveling at the speed of light, but since it has ingested its own tail, and since it has structural integrity, it is forced now to flow (at velocity c) in a circular path.

Bubble Rings: It is interesting that intelligent dolphins playing underwater are able to blow elongated bubbles into the water. These elongated bubbles are semi-stable and can be seen to be spirally twisting, and they look like (and are) a type of vortex. Then the dolphin quickly and expertly bends it into a circle with its snout, and the twisting tip joins with the twisting tail. The result is a twisting dancing 'bubble ring,' which can last a few seconds. This is not the same exact structure of an electron, but it's close enough to help make the concept of a stable twisting toroid more believable to the skeptic. It illustrates the *toroidal vortex ring concept* in a real life, everyday example. (If you google 'dolphin bubble rings' you will find videos of dolphins forming these incredible bubble rings).

Note please that the above discussion is a simplified first approximation which serves to illustrate the Aetheric flow pattern of an electron mass particle. Special relativity must ultimately be applied to the math to complete the 'observed' vector field pattern of the electron. Also, a mathematical mapping transformation will be needed to map the photon's [straight-path/cone-shaped/Euclidian-grid-based] *Aetheric Acceleration Vector Field pattern* onto a circle of the most stable size (e.g. of circumference equal to the wavelength of the originating photon).

Calculated size: As it turns out, this electron, with the above described 'toroidal' *Aetheric acceleration Vector Field*, is made from a very high energy gamma ray. According to Dr. Blaney's 2008 non-relativistic preliminary calculation, this gamma ray of light has a frequency on the order of 3.0×10^{42} cycles/sec, and a circle radius on the order of 1.6×10^{-35}m (note this is not the *radius of the electron* itself, which extends well beyond this core radius). This agrees with current published electron size estimates ($< 10^{-18}$m), since the preliminary calculated circle's radius is well under the whole-electron's size radius as it should be.

Ouroboros is life: This gamma photon which has been condensed into a toroidal-shaped electron mass particle can be symbolized by a snake curling around and eating its own tail. Interestingly, this image is often seen in various ancient texts. It has been called the 'Ouroboros,' and represents infinity or wholeness. In the author's view, **the Ouroboros represents the formation of matter**, which allows for the possibility of a new level of communication/information exchange – one that includes long term data storage, retrieval and exchange, such as occurs with DNA, leading to a new level of life, of consciousness, of evolving and of loving – a human life.

The *photon condensed into an electron* discussed above seems to also appear in a 20th century woodcutting by artist M.C. Escher, entitled *Spirals*. In it, he depicts a graphic drawing of a 'spiral form' traveling in a circle. It appears to represent an electron, in that it's twisted tip is flowing into its own twisted tail. It implies that the tip of the spiral will forever be circling within its own belly and tail, becoming trapped in the unusual geometry of its self-created, perpetual, twisting, black-hole-like tunnel.

In summary: The electron has an Aetheric acceleration flow pattern in which the photon, traveling in a circle, is sucked in to its own inwardly accelerating spiral flow, and as a result, the tip just keeps going around and around inside its own belly, appearing to flow mostly within a donut shape (mathematicians call this shape a toroid), all the while continuing to pull in the accelerating Aether from its surroundings, and all the while rushing around in a circle at the speed of light. This entity (the electron) will now be referred to as a form of 'condensed' light.

From a chemical engineering perspective, one would say that mass (i.e. an electron) is a different 'phase' of a substance, the substance being light. Free photons, when forced to flow in a circle (due to encountering regions of extremely high Aetheric acceleration/bent spacetime) 'condenses' onto/into itself.

When uncoiled DNA strands re-coil themselves up, they analogously condense onto themselves thus forming a different 'phase.' In all forms of condensation, even water vapor condensing to liquid water, and liquid water condensing to ice, the entities are held together in a stable condensed form via stable Aetheric accelerating Flow Patterns observed and measured as 'forces.' In other words, all the forces of the universe can be explained by the flow patterns of the Aether, as mathematically expressed in the Aetheric acceleration Vector Fields and the Aetheric Curl Vector Fields, as will be discussed in later sections.

Types of curvature: The Aetheric flow in the electron is more than just circular, however. It is both spiral *and* circular, giving two forms of curvature.

Some physicists like to pretend these curvatures are different dimensions, one 'dimension' being in the photon's spiral direction, and one in the electron's circular direction. There appears to be merit in using this view to achieve the most elegant mathematical forms. But the simplest to *visualize*, and the most realistic *Aetheric acceleration flow pattern of the electron,* can be accurately expressed in simple 3-dimensional space and time, with no extra dimensions needed. That is, it is most simply envisioned as an Aetheric fluid flowing spirally into a vortex, which is itself flowing into a circular path and becoming trapped (or entrained) in its own flow pattern.

There are two additional reasons, besides simplicity and elegance, to restrict our interpretation of 'light' and 'mass' as *Aetheric Acceleration Vector Fields in 3-D space and time* (and excluding extraneous dimensions).

Firstly, we *think* in three dimensions plus time, because it's the way our brain/nervous system stacks information, as pointed out by psychologist Robert Anton Wilson. So it is more satisfying and simple to think in 3-D plus time. It's like imagining a video.

Secondly, the spiral flow of the Aether (in the photon) *combined with its circular procession,* reminds us of a gyroscope. In fact, the gyroscopic nature of the *doubly-twisted Aetheric flow* of 'mass' is what gives mass it's measurable inertial properties – that is, it's resistance to movement. More discussion on this can be found at the following web pages posted 10/20/2008:

www.drcarolblaney.com
www.drcarolblaney.blogspot.com.

Note that in actuality, mass and light have *infinitely-nested gyroscopic properties*. This is due to the [fractally-nested curling and twisting of the ZPF at all size scales], of which mass and light are comprised. This in turn gives rise to corresponding *resistances to movement* from said *nested Aetheric acceleration Curl*.

The doubly-curling flow of the electron's Accelerating Aether, all confined to a very compact region of space, is what we observe as matter. The 'sucking-in-of-Aether' is no longer spread out across space, like it is in a photon; it is no longer diluted along the linear backbone of the photon zipping by, as it discretely sucks in the Aether – a little here, a little there – as it flies by faster than we can imagine (at the speed of light). Rather, in the electron, all the Aetheric influx is concentrated into a miniscule donut, and so the influx of Accelerating Aether is so great, so concentrated, that it appears to have 'mass', and appears to have a gravitational pull. This is because the electron's gravitational pull (that is, its influx of Accelerating Aether) is so concentrated and so great that it can actually be measured by our instruments and be observed with our telescopes (e.g. as planets orbiting stars, and as stars bending light), since planets and stars are made of electrons and other mass entities comprising [condensed light which accelerates the Aether into itself].

This gravitational pull is simply the inwardly accelerating flow of the Aether, which flows inwardly into the massive object (such as the electron, the planet, or the star) forever and ever. And the Aether accelerates into the electron in a spiral pattern that forever circulates (no longer in a straight line, but) in a circular path. Just like the photon, the electron has a gravitational pull. And just like the photon, the electron has an angular direction (a spin).

Spin: If the photon that makes up the electron is a clockwise photon (clockwise flowing Aether in the direction of the tip's flow), then the electron formed therefrom has clockwise properties. Escher's artwork of a 'self-imbibing' spiral depicts a counter-clockwise photon that has been formed (by our Archangel in the thought experiment) into a counter-clockwise electron.

Charge: The last point to make here is that a counter-clockwise electron will repel other counter-clockwise electrons, and be attracted to clockwise electrons (called positrons). This is because the flow direction of a clockwise electron will 'match up with' the flow direction of a counter-clockwise positron. That is, their *Aetheric acceleration Vector Field* vectors will be aligned. On the other hand, a clockwise electron will repel another clockwise electron, because their *Aetheric acceleration Vector Field* 'Arrows' oppose one another at close proximity.

This explains the nature of charge repulsion and attraction, and thus explains charge, and ultimately all of the forces of the universe, including the strong and weak nuclear forces. Gravity of course is just the raw inwardly flowing acceleration of the Aether into all vortices everywhere, and into all particles formed therefrom.

The reason a positron and an electron often annihilate one another (and release high-energy gamma rays) is that their geometry allows this to happen. They approach one another and superimpose upon one another until the new meta-structure is unstable, after which they become unlocked and fly apart. Their toroidal pathways are 'released' and the photons become un-trapped – that is, they are no longer condensed.

However, if the positron is *stably* joined with another positron and another electron, in a more complex flow pattern, then it will have a net positive charge, yet at the same time it will be geometrically unable to conform into the right position to annihilate (i.e. un-condense) another electron. These nuances of building the 'matter' of the universe from stable sub-atomic particles is the complex science of 21st century physics. However, in the present work we are merely pointing to the inner workings of such systems – that is, pointing to the *Accelerating Aetheric Vector Fields* – the 'fabric' of such systems.

Determinism or Indeterminism? It is left to the

mathematicians skilled in this field to actually calculate all the subatomic particles' approximate **Aetheric acceleration flow patterns**. Note that the word 'approximate' was used. The exact flow patterns can never be mathematically expressed in an exact manner, due to the infinitely nested flow nature of the ZPF of which all of our universe is comprised. To express it exactly, one would have to have infinitely nested equations, infinite time, infinitely intelligent computers, ad infinitum – The Mind of God, in other words. This parallels Heisenberg's uncertainty principal, expressing a similar statement but from a different perspective and context.

In the present work, we heuristically point to the tendency of Aetheric acceleration to form complex patterns that make up such mass 'entities' so that we may then proceed in utilizing this concept to direct the Reiki Energy. Reiki Energy is one and the same with this Aetheric acceleration, which flows into patterns that make up all light, all matter, and all life.

What causes all the physical forces of the Universe?

All the physical forces of the Universe are caused by the Aetheric acceleration Flow Patterns. The extent of the local bulk *Aetheric Acceleration Vector Field* determines the net gravitational force. At closer ranges, it is the direction (curl) of the entities' flow patterns, and specifically whether the Aetheric flows are opposed or aligned between entities, that determines the sign of the force (attraction vs. repulsion). The local magnitude of [both the 'acceleration' vectors and the 'curl' vectors of opposing entities] determines the nature of the force, whether it be electric charge, strong nuclear forces, or weak nuclear forces. Said another way, the size scale of the flow pattern determines whether the force is observed to be an electrical charge, a strong nuclear force interaction, or a weak nuclear force interaction.

Herein lies Blaney's theory of Unification.

What is Gravity?

Bulk Inwardly Accelerating Aether gives rise to the force we call Gravity.

As discussed earlier, the Aether is the fluid of the Universe which flows (accelerates) spirally inwardly, into patterns.   Aether accelerating into a stable vortex is light. Light that is circularly trapped in its own inwardly flowing Aetheric flow pattern is mass, and is a form of condensed light.

Both light and mass have inwardly Accelerating Aether that flows into them, and this is observed as a gravitational force. Mass has it's inwardly accelerating Aether so concentrated (into a tiny toroidal shape) that it's gravitational effect is easier to measure.

For example, Earth has so much mass, and thus so much Aether accelerating into its mass particles of which it is comprised, that the acceleration of Aether from outer space, into the Earth, is strong enough to hold us securely onto the Earth's surface. This is nothing new, and this was the realization that allowed Einstein to devise the General Theory of Relativity.

Fun tip #1: 'Warped spacetime' is a difficult and foreign concept to grasp unless you are a mathematician. The equivalent but easier-to-visualize concept of *accelerating Aetheric fluid* is used in this thesis, instead of the concept of warped spacetime, even though, mathematically, they are one and the same. The additional information provided by the *more 'visual' Aetheric acceleration point of view,* is that this view in fact acknowledges that Aether is a churning fluid, with non-zero viscosity, filled with Aether-inhaling Faerie Dust – that is, filled with sub-atomic gravitational particles popping into and out of existence.

This viewpoint is more accurate, useful, and elegant. It is more elegant because it is easy and straightforward for the human brain/mind to visualize an accelerating fluid that pulls objects along with it. In contrast, trying to visualize a purely mathematical concept called 'spacetime' is impossible, as can be seen in the myriad attempts to draw warped spacetime using curved blankets that do not properly illustrate the point. Also note that many naively use the term 'curved space' which is incorrect and misleading.

Fun tip #2: Note that while all the light photons on Earth do add to its gravitational effect (such as the light exchanged between chemical reactions in our bodies, the light emitted by light bulbs, and the 'black body radiation' emitted by all objects above absolute zero temperature and so forth), these photons have much less of a gravitational effect than the condensed light making up the mass of Earth and its biosphere.

What is electrical charge?

A large vortex formed into a circle, as seen in an electron and a positron, will give rise to charge attraction and repulsion, depending on whether the flows oppose one another (repulsion) or the flows reinforce one another (attraction).

Electron-electron repulsive force: Consider two electron mass entities each made from clockwise gamma photons. What happens when we bring these two electrons together? To answer the question, we look at the electrons *Aetheric Acceleration Vector Field*.

We can 'model' these electrons with a simple convenient qualitative model. Using two plain bagels, and using a felt tip pen, we can draw the clockwise photon's Aetheric flow pattern as a 'clockwise spiral' (clockwise in the direction of the photon's tip, which mimics the streamline of the Faerie Dust). In other words, using the felt tip pen, draw a small clockwise circle in the air repetitively. Then as you draw this clockwise circle, slowly move the pen forward, in the direction the photon will travel. This is the spiral shape you will draw, with arrows every inch or so, on the surface of the plain bagel. Do this all along the surface of the bagel. Repeat on the other bagel.

Next, when you take the two bagels and hold them close to one another, you will discover that no matter how you flip the bagels, the arrows will oppose one another by an angle around 90 degrees. This is a demonstration of how the Aetheric flow patterns of 2 electrons will cause repulsion.

Electron-positron attractive force: If you have a third plain bagel, you can make a model of a positron by drawing a counterclockwise spiral using a different color felt tip pen. You will discover that the bagels of differing color, one clockwise and the other counterclockwise, have arrows that align with one another. From a fluid dynamics perspective, these fluid flows reinforce one another and want to share the fluid flow, therefore they are attracted to one another. This is because *a closer proximity of the two entities* is a more desirable energetic state than when they are further apart.

Recalling the second law of thermodynamics, rephrased here: *All isolated fixed-energy systems naturally go to their highest entropy state.* In this case, the highest entropy state is the fixed-energy electron and the fixed-energy positron clinging to one another, thus requiring an external force to pry them apart (until the point when they merge into an unstable entity and transform back into their photon state). Here we are focusing *on the act of the electron and positron coming together.*

Of note: If the electron and positron are brought together in a particular configuration, they will actually merge into an unstable state and unlock their circular path, thus releasing two gamma photons.

This entire 3-bagel experiment can be done without bagels by considering that an electron (clockwise photon condensed into a toroid) and a positron (counterclockwise photon condensed into a toroid) are mirror images of one another, so naturally when you bring them close to one another, the arrows will naturally match exactly – as mirror images do. Note that in reality, the electron/positron pair, when they approach one another, will flip automatically into the most stable pattern, stacking like magnets do. Imagine bringing two magnets together, trying to force them together. They will automatically and naturally flip the correct way and then rush together. Electrons and positrons would be expected to stack tightly in an alternating pattern similar to how magnets stack – as long as there was a mechanism that prevented them from getting two close and merging into the unstable meta-state mentioned before.

A key point to remember in considering charge

repulsion and attraction as a phenomenon of the Aetheric acceleration Vector Fields of two approaching mass entities, is this. The magnitude and 'sign' – e.g. the direction – of the force is determined not only by the magnitude of the local Acceleration vector, but by its direction, and how much it acts with, or acts against, the other entity. The curl is also important, as it determines the size scale in which opposing (or additive) forces act.

What are the strong and weak nuclear forces?

These same attraction and repulsion phenomena seen in the electrical charges also give rise to the strong and weak nuclear forces, due to similarly aligned and/or misaligned Aetheric Acceleration Flow directions (vectors), albeit at progressively smaller size scales. For example, these closer-range forces occur from the fields of smaller-scale vortices and condensates therefrom.

What is dark energy?

The inward acceleration of the Aether into the ZPF vacuum of space (into the temporary, unstable whorls and vortices) gives rise to dark energy, which results in a net inward acceleration of the Aether into what might appear to be 'empty space.'

This gravitational effect (caused by the turbulent ZPF) is of a higher magnitude in the more turbulent regions of space (e.g. within galaxies and solar systems) where lots of movement and action is going on as planets and asteroids zip by and disturb the quiescent local Aether with their respective *Aetheric acceleration vectors* of considerable magnitude – much like disturbing a lake with lots of boats and water-skiers. There would likewise be less of a gravitational effect in the *less* turbulent regions of the ZPF, such as in regions between galaxies – much like a quiescent lake with few local disturbances.

This hypothesized statement – that there is more 'dark energy', more Faerie Dust, in the galaxies' interstices compared to the regions between distant galaxies, is supported by experimental findings. Scientists consistently report the existence of 'invisible matter' in galaxies that effects trajectories of large objects and causes higher-than-expected bending of light around the outer rim of said galaxies. It is the turbulent ZPF of the galaxy's belly, inhaling the Aether, that is responsible for this phenomenon.

Why is the Universe expanding?

All this inwardly accelerating flow of Aether, into light, into mass, and into the dark energy of the ZPF, has to be balanced by an equal and opposite flow, as stated by the first law of Thermodynamics: *Energy can be neither destroyed or created, only transformed.*

This enormous collective inward flow of accelerating Aether must, therefore, be balanced by an outward acceleration of Aether 'out there.' Aether is thus hypothesized to be accelerating both inwardly *and* outwardly. The Outwardly-Accelerating Aether will naturally carry with it anything in its path. This 'equal and opposite' balancing flow is hypothesized to create an ever-expanding universe.

This Aetheric Flux Theory's hypothesis is indeed confirmed via observations from the Hubble telescope which has observed galaxies flying away from us in every direction, and the further away they are, the faster they appear to be receding.

Application of Aetheric Flux Theory to Reiki:

In the context of Reiki healing, we now have all the information we need, in order to understand how the Accelerating Flow of Aether forms our light and all of the mass entities which make up the larger systems of our bodies and surroundings.

Next, let us contemplate what 'life' is, before we venture into our final analysis of how to perform Reiki healing with utmost effectiveness. This topic is discussed in the next chapter.

6 WHAT IS LIFE?

'Life' is an English word that is used to describe a condition or state that distinguishes animals and plants from inorganic matter, including the capacity for growth, reproduction, functional activity, and continual change preceding death.

In a book entitled *The Rainbow and the Worm: The Physics of Organisms,* contemporary physicist Dr. Mae-Wan Ho elaborates on the question 'What is Life?' Using her definition of life as a 'process of being an organizing whole,' she discusses numerous bodies of scientific research related to life, including non-equilibrium thermodynamics, coupled processes, coherent excitation, quantum optics, quantum entanglement, dynamic order, and life as a collective response to weak electromagnetic signals. It is the latter topic mentioned above, of life being a 'collective response to weak electromagnetic signals,' that are of interest tom the Reiki healer.

The term 'electromagnetic field' is a term used to describe a force that causes electrical current (e.g. electrons) to flow through a wire. Ultimately, electromagnetic fields are an observable phenomenon of the accelerating flow patterns of the Aether.

Weak electromagnetic fields are emitted by living beings, as well as from electronic equipment. Living beings emit bio photons as well as surges of Aetheric disturbances corresponding to blood flow, brain wave firings and heartbeats. The equipment used to detect these emissions are EEG (electroencephalogram) for brain nerve impulses, ECG (electrocardiogram) for heartbeat monitoring, and special cameras to detect bio photon emissions.

These Aetheric flow patterns throughout and around living organisms are much more complex, ordered, and information-packed than the fields around inanimate matter. These emitted permeate the organism, send messages throughout the organism, and orchestrate life.

How fast do these informational waves (perturbations of the Aether) flow throughout the body? The speed of movement of the pure quiescent Aether is instantaneous; on the other hand, the speed of light is finite, and is limited by the local Aetheric flux energy density (the turbulence of the ZPE). In free space we measure the speed of light to be limited to $c = 3 \times 10^8$ m/s. Light travels a bit more slowly when it travels through the dense medium of the human body, because the Aether through which it flows is denser and more turbulent there.

The body's natural, health-promoting, inter-communicating information-packed *Aetheric-based fields* are transmitted throughout the body at varying velocities, depending on the mode of transport. The speed of electrical current (via movement of charged particles) through the connective tissue, the fascia, is comparable to the speed of electricity through a wire. This is much slower than the speed of light, but still much faster than the speed of a hormone molecule traveling through a vein.

Light itself can send information throughout the body. High quantities of highly coherent infrared bio photons have been shown to be emitted from the hands of trained Reiki practitioners during healing sessions (James L. Oschman's book, Energy Medicine: the scientific basis). Also, infrared therapies are well-known to aid in tissue repair, blood flow, pain reduction and relaxation. These healing rays are thought to provide both informational and therapeutic effects to the healee.

What harms life?

There are good and bad electromagnetic fields (which are just Aetheric Acceleration flow patterns). We just mentioned good healing energy sent through the body (electrical flow through the fascia or light waves travelling through tissue, cellular and intracellular fluids). However, there is also a form of Aetheric acceleration-based information that is harmful to the health of the organism. Some forms of this Aetheric acceleration (this weak electromagnetic field) can add chaotic damage. Information transmitted through the Aether can be helpful or hurtful to life.

Example: If you are driving your car, and the radio informs you of a tornado in your area, you can safely drive away from it, and this is healthy, life-supporting information. However, if your radio station is telling a lie, and says the weather is clearing up, and in fact you drive towards a tornado, it is very harmful information. Lies are almost always destructive forms of information that are life-damaging.

What are some life-damaging forms of (Aetherically transmitted) information that are transmitted at the cellular level?

The harmful weak electromagnetic fields that bombard us every day are forms of 'lies' that lie to our bodies and give our bodies false information, and this results in our bodies doing the wrong thing, causing us harm to our overall health. These harmful fields are caused by dirty electricity, by the transformers we use for our tech devices, by our cell phones, from the currents in the walls, the electromagnetic disturbances from geomagnetic storms, and sometimes even the harmful electromagnetic fields emitted by angry or sad people around us.

Many researchers have reported cellular responses to these harmful weak electromagnetic fields, ranging from detrimental effects of cell phone signals and computers upon cellular metabolism, and also detrimental effects of human and animal well-being from geomagnetic storms. Poor lighting (such as rapidly flickering LED light) tells the pupils to rapidly expand and contract, causing eye pain. This is common when using LED-backlit computers, in which the screens are dimmed using pulse-width modulation. Even if the LED lights are set to not flicker, the color spectrum is lacking in red and infrared light waves, which are direly needed, in order to repair the constant damage caused by the blue light waves.

On the other hand, in natural sunlight (especially the early light and late afternoon light) the spectrum is very rich in red and infrared, allowing for rapid repair of the damage caused by higher energy blue-light. This is why true sunlight is always the best light, and incandescent lights are the next best thing, since incandescents are the only manmade light source that can mimic full spectrum sunlight. This is because the frequency distribution of incandescent light bulbs is continuous/smooth (like the sunlight) and is thus missing no colors.

In comparison, fluorescent and LED lights are hugely lacking in many specific colors, providing misinformation and incomplete nutrition to the human organism. This causes the destruction of health. The only reason some LEDs may seem to some to be full spectrum, is that the extremely narrow bands of red, green, and blue light they emit are adjusted in intensity to fool the eye's red, green, and blue cone cells into 'falsely perceiving' full spectrum when in fact it is not anywhere near full spectrum. However, the rest of the body is not receiving many 'colors' or frequencies of light that it needs for optimum health and well-being.

What helps life?

Positive effects upon life, from weak electromagnetic fields, include the therapeutic application of light to aid in wound healing, bone healing, circulation, detox, sleep improvement, and other aspects of healing. Such light therapy includes not only full spectrum sunlight for everyday nutrition and health, but also specific applications of colored light, ultraviolet light, and infrared light for various specific conditions. There are many light therapy products on the market that do this, including acne treatment, bilirubin lights for jaundiced babies, red and infrared light for joint pain reduction, far infrared saunas for rejuvenation and life extension, and brief ultraviolet treatment for boosting the immune system, to name a few.

The benefits of darkness at night time for good health is extremely important. The hormone that helps us sleep deeply is called melatonin. It is needed to protect against cancer, insure deep and healthy sleep, and insure our body is able repair tissue damage (which happens during sleep). Melatonin can only remain active when there is not any blue light present. Blue light causes any melatonin to vanish. That is why the *absence* of blue light at night insures melatonin formation. An hour before bed, lights should be dimmed, and cell phones, TVs and computer screens avoided, so that melatonin can be formed. If you need to use the rest room during the night, a dim red or amber night light is the healthiest choice. There are now many computer apps and cell phone apps that automatically redden the display an hour before your selected bed time. These are best used as a last resort. Some people use amber sunglasses before bed as a great tool to enhance melatonin formation.

As mentioned in earlier chapters, Dr. Oschman has measured high levels of coherent infrared light being emitted from the hands of trained Reiki practitioners during their healing sessions. Infrared has been quoted by NASA as being 'the healthiest of all rays,' and is needed for many life-promoting cellular functions.

Another phenomenon that helps life is positive intention, which is transmitted via the electromagnetic fields emitted from the healer. This is discussed in more detail in the next chapter.

In summary, good healing energies transmitted by *Aetheric acceleration flow patterns* include the following: natural sunlight, infrared light from the hands of Reiki practitioners, various light therapy devices, and full-spectrum incandescent light used as indoor lighting. Additional healing 'energy' comes from loved ones, pets, and nature, as well as a positive state of mind, since the mind/brain's intensions and thoughts effect one's own body more than anyone else's-.

Bad energies, which give the body false information or jumbled signals, cause cellular malfunction and damage the DNA, and include the following: EMFs from electronic equipment, non-incandescent lighting, unnatural environments, rooms filled with anxious people, cell phone towers and cell phones, transformers and electrical wiring, and the like.

7 RESONANCE, COHERENCE & INTENTION

In order for Earth Angels to send healing Reiki energy to others, they must understand two principles: (1) what healing energy is, and (2) how to properly direct it through the hands and into the healee. Item (1) was covered in the previous chapters. Item (2), how to direct this energy properly, will be discussed in this and the next chapter. First we must understand the concepts of coherence, resonance, and proper intention, since those are the states we must attain before we channel energy into the healee.

Brief summary of previous chapters:
We covered the basics of what Reiki Energy is – Accelerating Aether. This Aetheric Fluid Accelerates *into* you because you are made of 'gravitational' mass and light, and both mass and light are constructed of inwardly spiraling, inwardly accelerating, flowing

Aether. It accelerates *through* you because you are standing on the massive planet called Earth, and Earth is also made of mass and light, and is thus also constructed of inwardly spiraling, inwardly accelerating, flowing Aether which flows into the Earth, while dragging you along in its path, thus holding you in place.

Now, how do we channel and shape this Reiki Energy (Aetheric flux) while performing Reiki, in a way that can best support our healee?

Many people believe that you cannot hurt anyone with Reiki Energy, even if you perform it poorly. This is only partially true. If you perform 'incorrect' Reiki, you cannot cause disease, and you cannot cause any lasting damage to someone. But you could cause them agitation, which is not desirable. If you have very high standards and want to heal your client (or loved one) in the most effective way (providing no harm, and in fact providing powerful healing energy), you will want to learn how to optimize the energy that flows through you, into your client, in a way that prevents any 'agitating' energy from being transmitted.

We will begin with an example of how NOT to perform Reiki.

Resonance.
The worst mistake you can make is not taking the necessary time beforehand to prepare: to breathe deeply, center your mind, and attain a peaceful state.

This runs the risk of transmitting your negative (i.e. stressful) energy into your client.

Let's say you are performing Reiki on a client, and you are still angry at someone who yelled at you earlier that day. You may inadvertently send that anger energy into the healee, and if the healee is prone to feeling anger him/herself, then they could resonate quite easily in this 'anger' pattern. This will not help, and could agitate the healee. If the healee is an 'empath' (someone very sensitive to the moods of others), the anger could be transmitted and amplified – definitely not useful! In other words, they could become angrier than you.

One mechanism for this energy transfer includes your emitted electromagnetic field (comprised of *surges of patterned Aetheric Acceleration* analogous to radio waves) emitted from your beating heart, which contains biological information about your mood imbedded in its rhythmic pattern.

A simple metaphor follows. If the healee has a guitar string inside their body tuned to F#, and you sing a clear tone in the pitch of F#, that guitar string will begin to resonate in F# and soon ring loud and clear, the string itself generating more *F# sound vibrations* into the surroundings. Admittedly, this is a super-simplified analogy, but not too far removed from what really happens when you transmit 'anger' into someone prone to feeling 'anger.'

We have just discussed the phenomenon of

'resonance.'

When you prepare yourself properly before the Reiki session, you will then cease to send negative (chaotic, or otherwise non-useful) patterns to your healee, thus protecting them from resonating with these negative patterns. However, if you send positive patterns, such as good healing intention, love, caring attention, appreciation/gratitude and/or optimism, it can only help. Even if your healee does not easily resonate with the good 'vibes' you transmit, he/she will benefit from these vibes, since they promote coherence, order, and healing.

Coherence.
When your brain neurons all fire together at the same rate, your brainwaves will be coherent. This is seen when electrodes placed on selected regions of the scalp reveal electromagnetic fields with beautiful, repeating wave patterns of high amplitude and minimal chaos. Coherence implies the elements of the system are in communication with each other, and are behaving similarly. Expert meditators attain a high state of coherence because they have trained their mind-body systems to breathe slowly and deeply, to reach a state of peace and calm, and to be grateful and even blissful.

Intention.
When a human being forms a mental intention, it alters the pattern of Accelerating Aetheric energy flow in their body, and thus alters the field they emit and the pattern of Reiki Energy that their hands emit.

Without awareness of the effect of our thoughts and intentions on ourselves, others and the world, our energy output (if negative/harmful) can be misdirected, causing sorrow, pain or other forms of damage. This is why it is important to generate positive intention consciously, rather than let the chaos of life dictate our thoughts and intentions willy-nilly.

Author Lynn McTaggart interviewed many 'master intenders,' as she calls them, and reported their methods in her book *The Intention Experiment*. These methods are extremely useful to the Reiki practitioner, and for that reason her 'tips' are summarized below.

Tips to maximize and optimize your intention (in this case, to heal the client with Reiki Energy):

1. **Attain Alpha.** Quiet the mind by training yourself in meditation techniques, and attain the alert relaxed 'alpha' brainwave state, in which neurons fire coherently at 10-14 Hz. This is a very useful state to maintain for all of your Reiki healing. It ensures you are relaxed and peaceful. However, some practitioners use an additional, more advanced technique, when they feel called to do so, and it can be thought of as a form of prayer. It is discussed in the next tip.

2. **Attain Gamma.** After first attaining the

relaxed and alert alpha brainwave state and maintaining it a while, begin to now place all your mental 'oomph' into wanting, intending, and knowing that your client will be healed, and that you will be a compassionate channel for the optimum healing energy that is perfect for that person. When the 'master intenders' achieved this state of effective mental 'oomph' by generating feelings of compassion, their brain waves shifted from alpha (10-14 Hz) up to gamma (25-40 Hz). While it takes training to achieve this state, knowing *what it is* and *what to do to attain it* will go a long way to channel good, healing energy to your client. Wikipedia.org has this to say about gamma brainwaves as measured using EEG on trained, meditating Tibetan monks (emphasis is included by the author):

"Experiments on Tibetan Buddhist monks have shown a correlation between transcendental mental states and gamma waves. A suggested explanation is based on the fact that the gamma is intrinsically localized. Neuroscientist Sean O'Nuallain suggests that this very existence of synchronized gamma indicates that something akin to a *singularity* – or, to be more prosaic, a *conscious experience* – is occurring. This work adduces experimental and simulated data to show that what meditation masters have in common is *the ability to put the brain into a state in which it is maximally sensitive.*

"As mentioned above, gamma waves have been observed in Tibetan Buddhist monks. A 2004 study took eight long-term Tibetan Buddhist practitioners of meditation and, using electrodes, monitored the patterns of electrical activity produced by their brains as they meditated. The researchers compared the brain activity of the monks to a group of novice meditators (the study had these subjects meditate an hour a day for one week prior to empirical observation). In a normal meditative state, both groups were shown to have similar brain activity. However, when the monks were told to *generate an objective feeling of compassion during meditation*, their brain activity began to fire in a rhythmic, coherent manner, suggesting neuronal structures were firing in harmony. This was observed at a frequency of 25–40 Hz, the rhythm of gamma waves. These gamma-band oscillations in the monk's brain signals were *the largest seen in humans* (apart from those in states such as seizures). Conversely, these gamma-band oscillations were scant in novice meditators. Though, a number of rhythmic signals did appear to strengthen in beginner meditators with further experience in the exercise, implying that the aptitude for one to produce gamma-band rhythm is trainable.

"Such evidence and research in gamma-band oscillations may explain the heightened sense of consciousness, bliss, and intellectual acuity subsequent to meditation. Notably, meditation is known to have a number of health benefits: stress reduction, mood elevation, and increased life expectancy of the mind and its cognitive functions."

3. **Be loved and prayed for yourself** (if possible). It is interesting that Lynn McTaggart found that those prayed for themselves were more effective praying for themselves and others.

4. **Be centered, healthy, and peaceful** (if possible). Here we recall the importance of daily meditation, a reasonable lifestyle, sunshine, exposure to nature, proper food and sleep habits, and avoidance of unhealthy toxins (including unhealthy technology and unpleasant stress). Also, forgiveness techniques that help remove inner turmoil and provide inner peace can be found at the

following web page:
https://www.youtube.com/edit?o=U&video_i
d=nhgWyQzGAto

5. **Always practice in the same place** (or at least mentally imagine your optimum place, in a tranquil and safe setting)

6. **Practice 'intention' when geomagnetic activity is moderate**. McTaggart found intention effects to be more powerful when there was at least some geomagnetic activity (e.g. from sunspot activity). When geomagnetic activity was low, intention was less powerful, but psychic ability was stronger. Geomagnetic activity can be monitored each day at noaa.gov (on the space enthusiast dashboard). It won't always be possible to arrange to perform Reiki when geomagnetic activity is moderate, but for very important prayer work, distant Reiki, and self-healing work, it is good information to utilize.

7. **Make a connection to your healee/client**. It's very important to talk to the client first, look them in the eye, chat a while, discuss their concerns, even hold their hand (or shake their hand in a more formal setting). The more you can connect with them, the more powerfully the Reiki Energy will connect with them.

Now we are ready to teach how to channel coherent, resonant, and well-intentioned Reiki Energy effectively, using a step-by-step method, in order to insure your Reiki technique has healing benefits for the healee.

8 REIKI PRACTICE FOR ANGELS

There are four steps to insure that you, the Reiki practitioner, prepare yourself properly for the healing session, so that the channeled energy is pure, healing, and pleasant.

1. You must be mentally coherent
2. You must be physically coherent
3. You must be in a physically healthy environment
4. Your 'intention' should be optimized

To be **mentally coherent**, you will want your brainwaves to be coherent. This means that all the nerves are more-or-less firing together, indicating that all your mental facilities are in synch with one another. To attain this state, most practice some form of meditation. You'll know when you're coherent when you feel peaceful, grateful, calm, and loving. You will genuinely care about your client, the healee. Before and during the Reiki healing session, continually remind yourself to breathe in, and breathe out, in a slow, calm manner. Empty your mind of all chatter, focusing only on the client and his/her energy state, as well as your compassionate intention to help them in the most useful way possible.

To be **physically coherent**, you will want your body to be as healthy as possible. For many this means following a vegan diet, getting plenty of exercise and sunshine, and getting adequate amounts of restful sleep – especially before practicing Reiki. It also means abstaining from all unhealthy substances. Note: There are some people, such as type O blood types, who are not at optimum health without high levels of protein, and many claim to feel better with some meat in their diet. Nevertheless, it is advised that when a person does eat protein from animals, the person does so wisely. This means the person is conscious of, and grateful for, the sacrifice made by the animal. The person is also educated in, and diligent about, ways to source unpolluted meat as well as principals of proper food combining to insure good digestion/minimum toxin formation.

Deep breathing practice not only helps the mental coherence, as mentioned above, but helps the physical coherence as well. Deep breathing quiets the thoughts and thus supports information flow throughout the body, enhancing your own healing, well-being, and coherence.

To be in a **physically healthy environment**, you will need to perform Reiki in a quiet and private room with no interruptions. Ideally it would be a spare room in a home, in a tranquil neighborhood, and using halogen or other incandescent lighting, or even better, natural sunlight. Please never use any form of LED or fluorescent lighting.

A water fountain would be an ideal sound. Other sounds might include other nature sounds, flute, gentle guitar or piano. In all cases, the client/healee should approve the music. Please advise the client to speak up at any point if she/he would prefer the music be changed, since some pitches or rhythms can cause a person to tense up.

Shielding yourself from the negative energy of the client (as a precaution):
There are many methods taught by others on shielding yourself from negative energy fields, including imagining a large, mirrored 'bubble' around your body that reflects bad energy away and only lets in good loving energy. This can work if you are able to fully concentrate on it with ultimate focus, for a short time, e.g. when a brief event happens that you want to shield yourself from. But this method may not be practical or realistic during a 30-minute Reiki healing session.

A more powerful way to inhibit negative energy from entering your own field is to strengthen your own field with a lot of training in reaching a coherent state. Then, as you perform Reiki, as long as you remain coherent and concentrate on your own breathing and your own body sensations, occupying and 'owning' your body with power and worthiness, you will be shielded from the negative energy of others. This is because doing these actions strengthens your own field, thus making it less vulnerable to attack.

A **shielding practice exercise** to do, in order to train yourself to be strong and 'alive', making your own energetic field strong, powerful and impermeable, is as follows:

Owning Your Body:
Stand firmly on both feet, and breathe deeply and slowly. Focus on every part of your body one by one. For each part (for example hand, heart, knee) send feelings of appreciation to it for helping you live, and ask it to send you any information you need to help it have what it needs. Listen to it. Feel its aliveness. Be in that part of your body. Try to become aware of where that part of the body is, its shape, and density. Tense it, then relax it. Continue moving around in your body, covering as many regions as you can, and especially the areas in pain, or that otherwise cause you concern. In this way you are training yourself to be in your body, and to communicate with it, allowing your entire self to become whole, coherent, and one. As you progress in skill, be aware of more and more of your body parts at once. Ultimately you want to learn to quickly and habitually 'be fully in your

body' during the entire Reiki session, as well as wherever you go.

Before the session (while the client is preparing to lay down on the massage table):
This 5-minute period, in which you leave your client alone in the treatment room to prepare him/herself to receive Reiki treatment, is an extremely crucial time for you to prepare for the session. Below are offered a series of prayerful affirmations to say silently to yourself while practicing deep breathing and simple yoga stretches. You will want to tailor them to meet your own needs. The main point here is that your affirmations are to prepare you to be in a state of quietude, gratitude, and loving healing intention.

Reiki Preparatory Affirmations:

- Exhale as you hold your arms to prayer position over your heart, relax, close your eyes, and mentally say **"Let my mind be quiet, as in the beginning."**

- Now Inhale as you raise your arms high above your head, and mentally say, **"Let the divine manifest in all my sacred endeavors."**

- Again lower your arms to prayer position and say, **"May I be peaceful. May I be loving and loved."**

(Continue raising arms with each inhale, lowering them with each exhale.)

- Inhale: "May I receive the pure light of healing so I may help others heal."

- Exhale: "May I rise above my own suffering; for I know it is only an illusion. May I remember this always, and heal another with joy in my heart."

- Inhale: "May I appreciate all others for the lessons they teach me; for they help me to grow."

- Exhale: "May everyone, and my healee, be happy and free from suffering."

- Inhale: "May everyone, and my client, have peace in their hearts, and accept others as they are."

- Exhale: "From the heart of the Universe, may streams of pure light and pure nectar, which are made of the Aether, flow down and grant me energy and perfect information which I channel through my arms and hands to benefit both healer and healee."

The Reiki session:
Your client may sit or lie, on a chair, floor, bed, or (preferably) a massage table. The reason a massage table is most desirable is because you, the healer, will have the least amount of strain on your own body

(especially your back and neck) when your client's position is optimized for your height.

Summary of tips on how to optimize your healing intention (from Lynn McTaggart, *The Intention Experiment*):

To optimize your intention during the session, follow as many of the 7 tips given in the previous chapter as you can. They are summarized here:

1. Attain alpha (relaxed calm).

2. Optional: Attain gamma (compassionate healing intention). This is useful at appropriate moments in the session, to aid in releasing blockages or to do advanced energy healing, faith healing, prayerful support and the like.

3. Be loved and prayed for yourself if possible.

4. Be centered, healthy and peaceful.

5. Always practice in the same place when possible, or at least mentally recreate your optimal 'healing space.' An example is to imagine you are in a protected cabana at the ocean.

6. Practice compassionate 'healing intention' when geomagnetic activity is moderate for the most efficient effect.

7. Make a connection to your healee/client.

The healing session:

Perform Reiki on your client in the normal way, placing your hands over each key chakra area, head to toe, and then going back over the body as you are guided, based on the patient's concerns, your own practiced methods which you learned in your Reiki training classes, and your intuition.

As you perform Reiki therapy, you will not only be breathing in and out and remaining peaceful and centered, but you will also be imagining the Reiki Energy flowing into and through your body as you hold your posture in an optimum way as described below.

Posture:
Imagine a golden thread emerging out of the top of your head, as if you were a marionette puppet, and it is pulling upward on your head so that your spine is supported, supple, and upright (e.g. you are not slumping, strained, or otherwise compromising the flow of energy).

Conventional Reiki Master Level Practitioner techniques: Perform 'all over Reiki' as taught in your Reiki classes. Focus on specific areas of concern raised by your client, as you have been trained. Throughout the session, continue breathing in and out, intending that each breath provides you with the perfect energy and information to offer your client.

Reiki for Angels healing tips:
Below are various Reiki tools and tips to use as
needed during your session. Review them often, and
if you feel the need, please add your own personal
Reiki 'tools' to this list, on the pages at the end of this
chapter.

***Imagine the Reiki Energy pouring into you from
the sky, as an alive, glistening fluid filled with Faerie
Dust, sparkling and twinkling with rainbow colors.
Some of this living fluid is circulating into and
through all of your cells, and some flowing through
you and down into the Earth, grounding you.

***As you imagine this shimmering fluid flow, you
strongly intend that the flow patterns within your
body are synchronously orchestrating the optimal
healing patterns for your client. You imagine this
optimal healing pattern flowing out of your arms and
hands, into your client's body, carrying informational
energy to all the right places where it is needed.

***Visualize the excess or negative energy flowing out
of your client's feet into the Earth, grounding your
client. Imagine Earth as a vacuum cleaner pulling in
all excess/unwanted energy blockages, transforming
it with fire energy, into pure light.

***Engage all your senses as you perform this Reiki
technique. Imagine the client is feeling blissful, and
that they will feel much better that day, and that the

good feeling will last.

***Imagine that many people are thankful for your client, and generate your own gratitude for your client, and for all the wonderful things he/she has done over his/her lifetime to help others and the world. You shall exude gratitude and a sense of endearment to every living cell of this client, and feel appreciation for them, as if they were your beloved mother in a past life.

***Mentally ask the cells and organs of the client, 'How may I help you? What do you want me to know? What informational energy does your body need?' and be receptive to the response. If you like, imagine a spirit guide or angel beside you, guiding you and providing a flow of optimal energy through your arms and hands into your client. Imagining this scenario will facilitate the energetic information transfer.

***If the patient has shared his mental anguish, send silent intentions that the client will soon find answers and meaning to their trials and tribulations. When you hold your hands over them, silently say, "I send you the pure light of peace. The universe loves you. It appreciates you. You have a wonderful purpose here and you are loved, appreciated and needed. You are so wonderful, like a fresh flower. I see that pure flower, and I want you to see that pure flower too, fresh and beautiful, just as you were meant to be. You are wanted on Earth. You are so worthy, so needed, and so many can benefit from you being here. Please see this.

***Over each region that you lay your hands, mentally affirm one or more of the following:

- May my body, speech and mind be in perfect oneness.
- I send my pure heart along with the light information, through my hands
- May you, the healee, awaken form your forgetfulness, and transcend the path of anxiety and sorrow, illness, pain, or power-seeking.
- I send you pure light from heaven. Please accept my gift; may you benefit.
- May your mind become quiet and listen to your body. May your mind love and honor your body, and all the world too. May your mind and body love the world and offer peace.
- I send you each beautiful color of the rainbow, and may each color fill you with peace, joy and love. May you feel loved and loving.

***Use standard Reiki methods to purge toxic energy from the painful areas of the body. It is also helpful to silently address each toxic energy body that you are about to purge from the body, by speaking to the toxic energy body as follows: "Hello little voice in there. I see you. I honor you. I see that you feel pain and sorrow. Yes, I understand that you are suffering. I wish you peace. I wish you well. Goodbye my friend. It is time now to go to sleep. You are OK, and you are safe now. Sleep well, my little friend." -- and then after you pull out the energetic body and send it into the Earth, wave your hands over the body to erase its suffering. Next, you will want to replace the removed blockage with positive energy. You can imagine a pink rose, or use a rose quartz crystal in your hand, pouring pure love in the 'hole.' Then it will be time to help 'seal the energetic hole' by waving your hand in a spiral pattern over the hole, sealing it securely in your mind and with your intention.

Ending the Reiki Session.
As taught in your Reiki classes, run your hands from head to toe in large sweeping motions a few times to complete the session, as you say softly that the session is almost done.

Communicate how much time is available for the client to remain alone in the room alone before the session officially ends.

While your client is left alone, it is a good time to wash your hands, drink water, and breathe deeply in solitude to ask your body how it feels.

Afterwards, let the client share their experience with you if they are moved to do so. Please continue to feel gratitude and appreciation for them as you (or they) leave.

After the session:

Cleansing leftover negative energy.
After a healing session, to be safe, it is normal practice to wash your hands with soap as you imagine all negative energy leaving your hands, body, and mind. Even better (if at all possible), a full shower is recommended to insure complete purification after a healing session is complete. A glass or two of water is recommended as well.

Ask your own body if it needs anything more.

If you perform Reiki many times in one day, at least plan a shower at lunchtime and another at the end of the work day. From a scientific perspective, water is a conductor, and serves to neutralize, absorb, and remove any excess electromagnetic energy. Water also *shields* you from incoming fields, allowing your own field to calmly regenerate itself without negative interference from outside influences, be they from electronics or people.

Last word:
We are all part of one giant energy field, and every part has an effect on every other part at every moment. Objects are not separate. All objects, organisms, and systems are defined by flowing Aetheric patterns that extend outwardly forever and in all directions. And we are all co-creating our environment and ourselves every time we observe or perceive our world. That is why Reiki works.

We can help co-create coherent, life-promoting, love-promoting Aetheric Fields by following methods taught in this book, and by living life consciously.

Peace.

Reader's notes and personal Reiki Tips:

C.A. Blaney, Ph.D.

ABOUT THE AUTHOR

C.A. Blaney is a Ph.D. Theoretical Chemical Engineer specializing in Fluid Dynamics and Thermodynamics. Using her natural and trained ability to visualize fluids flowing in 3-D space and time, Blaney was able to offer a new 'Fluid Dynamics' view of Physics that unifies all the physical forces of the Universe. Blaney's ongoing interest in metaphysics lead her to study Reiki and apply her new theories to better understand and utilize Reiki Energy to heal her loved ones. Her work is a direct extension of Einstein's ceaseless search for a Unification Theory, in which Blaney combines Einstein's General Theory of Relativity with Fluid Dynamics, providing a way to easily visualize the Aether's flow at very small and very large size scales. This ability to visualize the flows makes it possible to comprehend all the forces at play in our Universe, including the force of charge attraction and repulsion, the weak and strong nuclear forces, gravity, as well as explaining dark matter and an expanding universe.

Dr. Blaney, a native Texan, has lived in Houston, Mexico, Delaware, Georgia, Ohio, Oregon, and currently resides in British Columbia with her beloved husband.

Alice Bailey, describing the fabric of space:

"Esotericism teaches, and modern science is rapidly arriving at the same conclusion, that underlying the physical body and its comprehensive and intricate system of nerves, is a vital, or etheric, body, which is the counterpart in the true form of the outer intangible phenomenological aspect. It is likewise the medium for the transmission of force to all parts of the human frame, and the agent of indwelling life and consciousness. It determines and conditions the physical body, for it is itself the repository and the transmitting of energy from the various subjective aspects of man, and also from the environment in which man (both inner and outer man) find himself."

...

"The individual aetheric body is not an isolated and separated human vehicle, but is, in a peculiar sense, an integral part of the aetheric body of that entity which (we), the channeled teacher, have called 'the human family.' This kingdom in nature, through its etheric body, is an integral part of the planetary etheric body. The planetary etheric body is not separated from the etheric body of other planets, but all of them in their totality along with the etheric body of the sun, constitutes the etheric body of the solar system."

Made in the USA
Columbia, SC
07 November 2017